O CANADA
C R O S S W O R D S
B O O K 8

O CANADA

CROSSWORDS

BOOK 8

BARBARA OLSON

DAVE MACLEOD

75 Themed Daily-Size Crosswords

NIGHTWOOD EDITIONS

Nightwood Editions.
773 Cascade Crescent
Gibsons, BC
V0N 1V9
www.nightwoodeditions.com

Nightwood Editions acknowledges financial support from the Government of Canada through the Book Publishing Industry Development Program and the Canada Council for the Arts, and from the Province of British Columbia through the British Columbia Arts Council and the Book Publisher's Tax Credit.

Library and Archives Canada Cataloguing in Publication

O Canada crosswords.

Bk. 8 written by Barbara Olson and Dave Macleod.
Later books in the set published by Nightwood Editions.
Contents: Bk. 1. 115 great Canadian crosswords – bk. 2. 50 giant weekend-size crosswords – bk. 3. 50 more giant weekend crosswords – bk. 4. 50 incredible giant weekend crosswords – bk. 5. 50 fantastic weekend crosswords – bk. 6. 50 great weekend-size crosswords – bk. 7. 50 wonderful weekend-size crosswords – bk. 8. 75 themed daily-sized crosswords.

ISBN 1-894404-02-5 (bk. 1 : pbk.).—ISBN 1-894404-04-1 (bk. 2 : pbk.).—
ISBN 1-894404-20-3 (bk. 5 : pbk.).—ISBN 0-88971-206-9 (bk. 6).—
ISBN 0-88971-218-2 (bk. 7).—ISBN 978-0-88971-217-1 (bk. 8)

1. Crossword puzzles. 2. Canada—Miscellanea. I. Olson, Barbara, 1963– II. Macleod, Dave, 1951– III. Title.
GV1507.C7H35 2000   793.73'2   C00-910576-X

Printed in Canada

Contents

1   À la Carte

ACROSS

1 Lenin's country, initially
5 Father's sons: Abbr.
8 Elect
14 Desktop item
16 "Birmingham" singer Marshall
17 FISH
19 Prized violins
20 Quick trip
21 Go soft, in a way
22 Are enraged
23 Add-on at the till
26 BEEF
30 Chem. pollutants
34 AOL, e.g.
35 *The Beachcombers* role
36 Green sailor's lack
38 On the ___ (furious)
40 Crook's handle
41 "Scram!"
42 Investigate, with "out"
43 CHICKEN
47 Second degs.
48 "Ladies dancing" number
49 "The stump of ___ he held tight in his teeth . . ."
54 Atlantic peninsula
56 Hunk of mythology
57 LAMB
61 Colours slightly
62 Hot and bothered
63 Waiter's words of relief
64 LCD monitor's lack
65 Tchaikovsky's ___ *Lake*

DOWN

1 Release a deadbolt
2 "Ditto"
3 Classroom threat, once
4 French income
5 Pleasures
6 CD ending
7 Eddie the Eagle's Olympic event
8 Holds dear
9 Future sign
10 Like sour grapes
11 Env. insertion
12 "What can ___ for you?"
13 Cat tail?
15 ___ *John Malkovich* (1999 film)
18 Genie's home
22 To-do
23 Rice dish: Var.
24 Shows rage, as a llama
25 PC pros
27 Oil patch sight
28 Sound from a cranky canine
29 Sales agts.
30 ___ 23 ("The Lord is my shepherd . . .")
31 Ben Jonson dedicatee
32 Tries to stay afloat
33 Kill, à la fairy tale
37 Immigrant's subj.
38 Telegram
39 Supped
41 Relative to relatives
44 Stay firm
45 First-class fliers, often
46 Toddlers' pops
50 Hardy, Hope and Hood
51 Newlywed's gain
52 "La ___" (Virgin Mary depiction)
53 German industrial hub
54 "Goo-goo" go-with
55 Thumbs-up votes
56 At the drop of ___
57 Homer's H
58 Do nothing
59 Early show for Aykroyd: Abbr.
60 Train co.

2 *Game Misconduct*

ACROSS

1 Asset for a politician
9 Start of a Beatles title
15 Unduly suspicious
16 Short stops
17 Start of a hockey quip
19 Lyricist Gershwin
20 Plumber's tool
21 007, for one
24 Word form for "outer"
25 CEO's degree
28 Ornamental vase
29 Jazz job
32 It has many layers
34 Outlying
35 Bid ___ farewell
37 Rime
38 More of the quip
42 Singer Falana
43 GM Place or the Saddledome
44 Start of many French titles
46 Not on the up-and-up
49 Part of KPH
50 Get to
51 ___ *Kapital* (Marx)
52 The U of UBC
54 Sucker
56 Barrel part
57 N'est-ce ___?
58 End of the quip
65 Poker declaration
66 Small, as a town
67 Big name in beer
68 Paces off

DOWN

1 Kirk or Hook rank: Abbr.
2 Derisive laugh
3 "Is" in another form
4 "I'm ___ to go!!"
5 Neon or helium
6 Homer king Sammy
7 60 secs.
8 Amount of one's own medicine
9 It'll knock you out
10 Consider reliable
11 Minstrel's instrument
12 Enzyme suffix
13 Goddess, to Gaius
14 An end to alcohol and sex?
18 Shallow, like a birdbath
21 "___ Wiedersehen"
22 It's available in bars
23 Registers
25 Like a romantic evening
26 Old straw hats
27 Taxing mo.
30 "___ Had a Hammer"
31 Live like a local
33 Revolutionary Guevara
36 Big maker of ATMs
39 Figure skater Babilonia
40 Suffix with hero
41 Roads to conflict
42 It may be flipped
45 Snowbird's milieu
47 Pick of the litter, usually
48 Sulking
53 Rattler's defence
55 ___ *Like It* (Shakespeare)
56 Sect in Iraq
57 Arraignment offering
58 The Everly Brothers' "___ I Kissed You"
59 Man-mouse connector
60 Bar pickup
61 It makes a man mean
62 "It's c-c-cold!"
63 Suffix with verb
64 Cancels, in a way

■ BARBARA OLSON

3 *Capital Ideas*

ACROSS

1 More ample
7 Mock words of understanding
11 Indian title
14 Peter of *The Stunt Man*
15 Snakes that'll put the squeeze on you
16 A Bobbsey twin
17 Money raised by Girl Guides?
19 Spirits stat.
20 She'll rub you the right way
21 Part of a common palindrome
22 Red start
24 Calgary-to-Edmonton dir.
25 ___ takes is one bad apple
26 Word with up or down
27 Canadian $50 bills?
29 Non-committal reply
31 Days of rest
32 HBO competitor
34 A ___ (yours: Fr.)
35 Cliff climber's grip
40 Make out
45 Lottery winner's celebration?
47 ". . . through the air with the greatest of ___"

48 Kook
49 Prefix meaning muscle
50 Parkay products
51 German Sommer
52 Gingerbread goo
54 WWII carrier
55 Birthday dessert that's filled with money?
58 Grass skirt go-with
59 Plough pullers
60 Flashy fish
61 Bill encl.
62 Dodo or emu
63 Feudal tenant

DOWN

1 Rapper Tone ___
2 ___ Z (the gamut)
3 Maximum number in the kitchen, say
4 Kids' racers
5 "I Still See ___" (*Paint Your Wagon* song)
6 Canadian rugby star Gareth
7 Is plentiful
8 Furniture wrecker, maybe
9 Poultry seasoning
10 ___ Kosh clothing
11 Get growly with
12 Renaissance writer Sir Walter

13 Gets going
18 *North of 60* Native band
21 Part of a common palindrome
22 "It ___!" ("Look at me!")
23 Saturday night live grp.?
25 1960s radical Hoffman
27 Wash the floor again
28 "If ___ meet . . ."
30 Prefix meaning race
33 Loud American crowd member
35 *The Time Machine* writer
36 Asian saltwater lake
37 Moore's purchase
38 Messier move
39 Seasick sailor's refuge
41 Decides on
42 Cocktails served with a celery stick
43 Classical group of Sask.
44 "Right on!"
46 Sans flaw
50 Milo of *Barbarella*
52 Augustus' 1111
53 "Take off, eh?" show
55 Break down
56 Kipling snake
57 Night sch. course

4 *Black & White*

ACROSS

1 Volcano on Sicily
5 Stir up, as a fire
10 The centre of Czechoslovakia?
14 Landlord's notice
16 Nothing to the French
17 They're black & white
18 Ultimatum word
19 "Yer ___ luck"
20 Salute of a sort
21 Demure
24 Barely a team
25 City on the Clyde
27 Not refined
29 Muffin stuff
30 Antacid brand
31 1-Across shape
32 Knitted thing
34 It's black & white
38 Impulse conductor
39 Stable mother
42 Word that often precedes "show time"
45 Bugs in lines
46 Out to pasture, in a way
48 Bar ___ (ceremony)
50 Actress Farrow
51 Beaufort, for one
52 "Gay" city
53 Queen, worker, or soldier
55 Graceful horse
56 It's black & white
61 Animal house
62 Quest for Marco Polo
63 "¿Cómo ___ usted?"
64 Turkish coins
65 Pique

DOWN

1 East ender
2 Wing-tip part
3 At once
4 Schoolyard retort
5 It may be a bust
6 ___ bottom
7 Olive genus
8 Plop preceder
9 They're not from around here
10 They're black & white
11 Fodder
12 Workbook unit
13 Boxer's sequence
15 Veggies in a sack
20 Patty Hearst's alias
21 Nero's perfect 10-pin score?
22 Tic-tac-toe win
23 Canuck neighbour
25 Adult
26 It may get plastered
28 This pulls a bit
29 Urban sections, for short
32 Railroad bed
33 Fredericton's stately trees
35 Depart
36 Moon goddess
37 Diner sign
40 Have misgivings about
41 Child-care writer LeShan
42 Skewer
43 Bejewelled headwear
44 Juan de Fuca is one
46 Bridal paths
47 One of 15-Down by another name
49 It's black & white
50 Miata maker
53 Industry magnate
54 They're sometimes bruised
56 Old TV's ___ Club
57 Mentalist Geller
58 Hose wrecker
59 "Lord, is ___?"
60 RCMP rank

5 *Crowd Noise*

ACROSS

1 Lanchester and Martinelli
6 Q-Tip, for one
10 Go for ___ (get wet)
14 Civil servant of a sort
16 Iditarod terminus
17 With 58-Across, warning in a crowd
18 Machu Picchu Indian
19 Stay out of sight
20 Feature of some 'Vettes
21 With 52-Across, warning in a crowd
25 Post-CCF
26 Off-limits
27 Persians, now
29 Derisive laugh
31 Days of yore, in days of yore
32 Cash for 27-Across
33 Sound investment?
36 Warning in a crowd
40 Child of Chibougamau
41 Gun, as an engine
43 Batt. terminal
46 Tic-tac-toe loser
47 Fix the floor or roof
48 Squirrel snack
50 Baseball stat.
52 See 21-Across
53 Confident
54 Funny girl Goldberg
57 Fake coin
58 See 17-Across
63 Cry at an unveiling
64 Where to find a power plant
65 Pitcher Hershiser
66 Understands
67 Camp sights

DOWN

1 One of eight Eng. kings
2 Mauna ___
3 Pepper or Snorkel: Abbr.
4 Svgs., for one
5 Satirist Mort
6 Where you'll see a TBA notice
7 Sassy kid
8 Bubbly chocolate
9 Witch's concoction
10 Singer Baker
11 With 45-Down, warning in a crowd
12 "That's okay with me"
13 Chinese cuisine veggie
15 Special delivery?
21 Prefix with life or wife
22 Copy-machine insert: Abbr.
23 Barn topper
24 Maternally related
26 "And ___ off!" (horse race call)
28 Type of patch
29 Test the weight of
30 Escort's offer
33 1960s soul record label
34 Won ___ soup
35 Borrow from
37 Tabloid subject
38 Tel ___
39 Kind of log
42 Part of KPH
43 Be inherited by
44 Eye-related
45 See 11-Down
47 Reach maturity
49 Fit for a king
50 Compact item
51 Mr. Karloff
54 Forks in the road
55 Sharpen
56 "___ the Blues When It Rains"
59 Mined-over matter
60 Cyclotron bit
61 Modern denial
62 Hockey bigwigs: Abbr.

6 *Club of Jacks*

ACROSS

1 Jack's dietary restriction
6 Stalactite site
10 Chief Greek god
14 ___ *Gay* (WW II plane)
15 Opposed to, in the boonies
16 Sicilian smoker
17 Leeway
19 Tucks in at night?
20 Old French coin
21 Jack's has a hot tip
23 All full
25 Stallone, briefly
26 Star Wars mil. project
27 What Horton hears
29 Utterance when the light goes on
32 "___ boy!" ("Well done!")
35 Squat
37 Home buyer's needs, often: Abbr.
39 Jack's self-congratulatory comment
42 Too, in Terrebonne
43 ___ Minor
44 Secret opening?
45 A mi. has 1760
46 Tiny tick
48 Flin Flon-to-Winnipeg dir.
50 Green machine
51 *Shall We Dance?* co-star
55 Jack's quest
60 Loud noise
61 Look: Lat.
62 Toy gun sound
64 Meat of the matter
65 Düsseldorf donkey
66 Gibberish
67 McGwire home-run rival
68 Blunt-tipped weapon
69 Jack's much-loved kind of candy

DOWN

1 Less dated
2 TV's *Stars* ___
3 Get steamed
4 Math division: Abbr.
5 Applied powder
6 Mexican meat
7 "Yes, there is ___!"
8 Six-stringed instrument
9 Catch in a net
10 Piquant
11 Sewing case
12 Like a jokester at a funeral, for short
13 Moose Jaw's prov.
18 Causing worry, with "at"
22 Replay mode
24 Future atty.'s exam
27 Be gaga over
28 Rolls of dough
29 Big Turks
30 Sews up
31 ___ stands (currently)
32 "You've Got ___" (Shania Twain song)
33 Fall sound
34 Soviet news service
36 Month before *école* starts
38 Aggressive, personality-wise
40 Intend on
41 *Fred* ___ (comics canine)
47 Escapee's cry
49 Backpack features
50 Ex-NDP head McDonough
51 "And thereby hangs ___"
52 Pound hound's lack, often
53 Rodeo rope
54 Key above Shift
55 They're above the abs
56 Height: Prefix
57 MDs' milieux
58 Yellow jacket
59 Done to ___
63 1990 Capote stage-bio

7 *The Colour of Money*

ACROSS

1 Hay bundler
6 Traveller's destinations, at times
10 CD part?
14 Stop on ___
15 Jacob's first wife
16 Humorist Bombeck
17 Allowed, as evidence
19 Pen end?
20 Sudbury-Toronto dir.
21 Limerick's land
23 Church council
25 *Swan Lake* legwear
26 Like Disney's films
28 With 41-Across, this puzzle's theme
30 Serves dinner to a bunch of pigs
31 Flutter one's eyelids, say
32 "___ Beso" (hit by 49-Down)
35 Moving vehicles
36 Happy and sad
37 Pudding fruit
38 Fest in the West
39 Open with a racket
40 ___ fatale
41 See 28-Across
42 Drinks daintily from
43 Big oaf

46 In a tizzy
47 Peacemaker's offering
50 Blue Jays stat.
53 Singer Tennille
54 Advice giver
56 Fort site
57 A wet body
58 Children's song refrain
59 Canucks stat.
60 Bar-goer's pass it?
61 "I'll count ___" (parent's threat)

DOWN

1 Kids' talk
2 Puts two and two together
3 Rock found notably in Kingston, Ontario
4 RCA rival
5 Emails again
6 Perjurer's confession
7 State north of Kan.
8 Simba's sweetie
9 Lean-tos
10 Spirograph user's output
11 Like many St. Patrick's Day celebrants
12 Young salmon
13 Sticks in Grandma's closet

18 It hangs heavy in the air
22 Try to take off?
24 Informal agreements
26 Invitation letters
27 "The Eagle" Eagleson
28 Fingered clothing
29 Midway feature
31 Mustang maker
32 Setting of a Wes Craven horror film (1984)
33 Wrestling in Japan
34 Red sky in the morning, e.g.
36 Spaghetti topper
37 Blanc's Le Pew
39 Feathered editor of comics
40 Sexy stocking style
41 Part of the USSR
42 Pet rescue grp.
43 Must, hastily
44 "Zut ___!"
45 Stage deliveries
46 Still for rent
48 Genetic strands
49 "Put Your Head on My Shoulder" singer
51 Creamy cheese
52 "The Heat ___" (Glenn Frey tune)
55 Roman god

8 *Turn Up the Heat*

ACROSS

1 Libra feature
8 Was in a row
15 Newspaper issue
16 One who won't give up
17 CO$_2$ and methane
19 Seine feeder
20 Menu phrase
21 Pretzel topper
22 Keanu's role in *The Matrix*
23 Ski-hill transports
25 Bay St. takeovers
28 The blahs
30 Presupposed
33 Some radios, for short
35 After-lunch sandwich
36 Dead letters?
37 What 17-Across might cause
41 Arthur of *The Golden Girls*
42 Novelist Turgenev
43 Bub
44 Golden-ager
46 Chicks' hangouts
50 "___ sow, so shall . . ."
51 *The Count of Monte Cristo* author
55 Discovery cry
56 Org. searching for signals from space
59 Like steak tartare
60 One-time African despot
61 What 37-Across might cause
65 Snared
66 Words after "bring" or "in"
67 Spanish guys
68 They're often slo-mo

DOWN

1 Shakespearean "Get lost!"
2 Arpel of cosmetics
3 Rests atop
4 Precisely, after "to"
5 *Delta of Venus* author
6 Roommate, briefly
7 Reflected alone?
8 BC Lions scores
9 Turnabouts, slangily
10 Nintendo rival
11 "Want me to?"
12 Youngest of the family
13 Prior to, to Prior
14 Driller's degree: Abbr.
18 Former Mideast org.
23 Popular donut hole
24 Poet Teasdale
26 Not a dup.
27 Sample, as soup
29 Sci-fi sighting
31 Salon job
32 Caesar's subjects
34 Goal for goalies
35 Part of B.Y.O.B.
37 Hair goops
38 Role for a Hollywood hunk
39 Fat in a can
40 Glaciers, mostly
41 Fluffy scarf
45 "It would ___ me . . ."
47 Winged maple fruit
48 Age at which trust was lost in the '60s
49 Hitachi rivals
52 Catering dispenser
53 Blair was his heir
54 Well-apprised
57 Part of NWT: Abbr.
58 Requiem Mass word
60 *Clan of the Cave Bear* author
61 Bro's sib
62 One, in Verdun
63 VCR speed measure: Abbr.
64 Broadbent's party: Abbr.

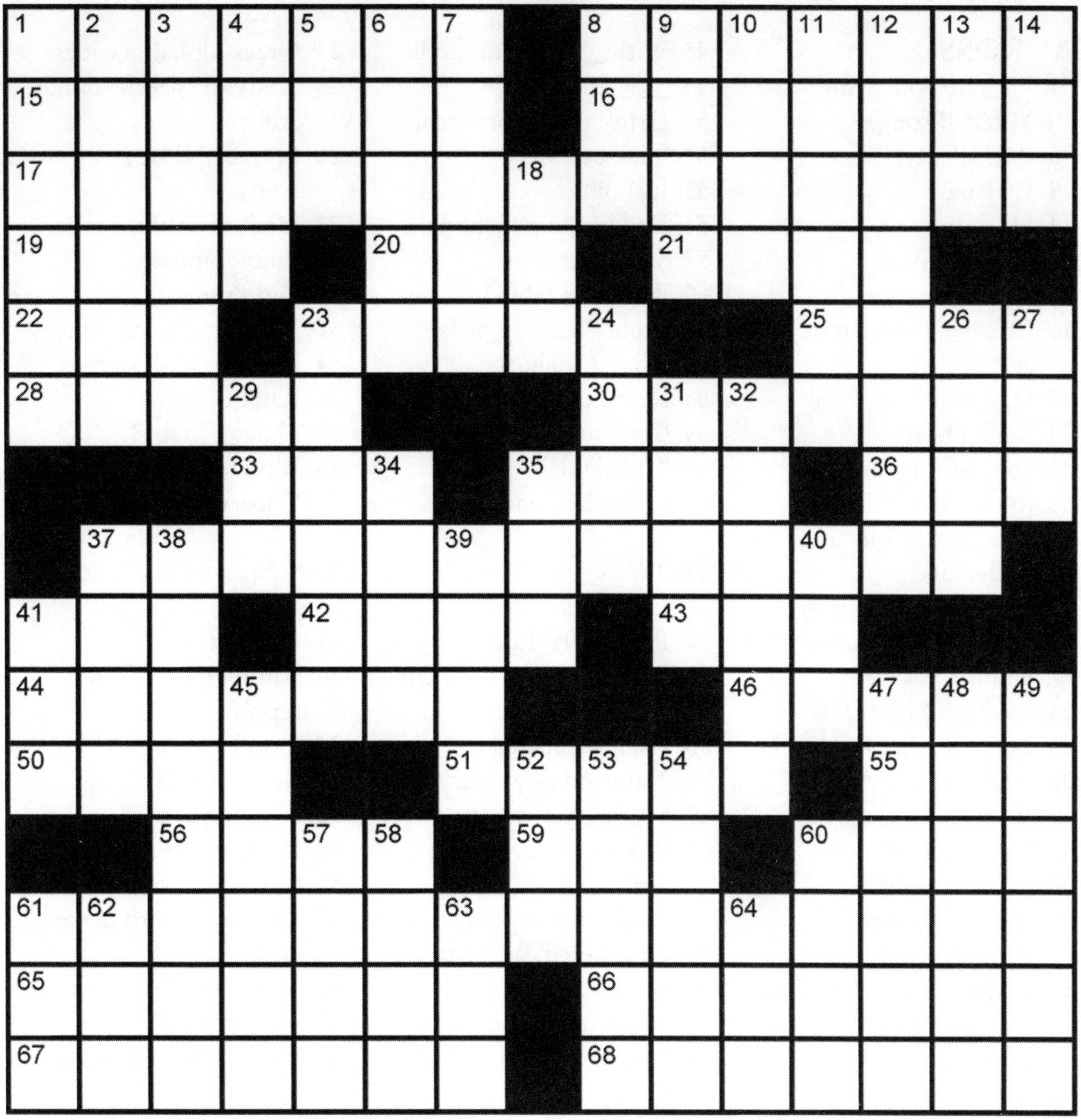

9 *Cowboy Humour*

ACROSS

1 "___ of You" (Joni Mitchell song)
6 RCMP alert
9 GST part
14 Ho-hum, as a performance
15 Actress Joanne
16 Cop ___ (bargain in court)
17 Hail Marys, in Latin
19 Belle's beau
20 Start of the punchline to this joke: Why did the cowboy buy a dachshund?
22 "___ tu" (Verdi aria)
23 Words before roll or whim
24 Soul of Québec?
25 24 Sussex Dr. residents
28 Step down, maybe
30 Wise one
32 Captain's call
33 ___ in "apple"
35 Mountains near Revelstoke, BC
37 Middle of the punchline
40 Australia's capital
41 Camera type: Abbr.
42 Good points
43 VHS predecessor
45 With ___ of thousands
49 ___ Tin Tin
50 Drink served on a trolley
51 Stick up
53 Just out
54 End of the punchline
57 Simple to do
60 Reserve a table for one
61 Santa's landing pads
62 Alias, for short
63 Rent out again
64 Cozy and snug
65 "All right!"
66 Cherished ones

DOWN

1 Degrades
2 Prance playfully
3 Red blood cell deficiency
4 "Ditto"
5 Highly detailed
6 Name on a sweater?
7 Say 17-Across, say
8 React to sidesplitting humour
9 Butler portrayer in film
10 Uncovered, in verse
11 Schnozz ending
12 Some, along the Somme
13 Emulated Miss Muffet
18 Don's hockey-talking sidekick
21 Greek alphabet enders
25 Study of speech sounds: Abbr.
26 Former NHL goalie Andy
27 Method: Abbr.
29 Pound units?
31 Didn't miss ___
32 Multiple choice choices
34 Fruity iced dessert
36 Rail call
37 Mata ___ (spy)
38 Wise to
39 Cheery cashier's wish for you
40 Subject of *The National Dream*
44 Icy spots
46 Southwest African republic
47 Trawler
48 Birds' words
50 Blowing over?
52 Dedicated work
54 Cartoonist's guffaw
55 Common word in teen-talk
56 Singer's club
57 Slo-pitch ball's path
58 Actor Jack of *Barney Miller*
59 ___ de plume

10 *Turn Me Loose*

ACROSS

1 Fill-up fluid
4 Cloud layers
10 Kiln for hops
14 Tin Tin opener
15 ___-Dazs ice cream
16 They may be put in stitches
17 Latin lover's word
18 With no profit
19 Faucet fault
20 Nailed red-handed
23 Caesar's words to Brutus
24 Util. bill
25 Chronic complainers
27 Title for Godiva
29 Weapons supply
31 Self expression?
32 Apt. with no windows, perhaps
33 Prince ___ Khan (who married Rita Hayworth)
34 Retired from the rodeo circuit
39 SASE, for one
40 Tiff
41 Mme. across the Pyrenees
42 Painting genre
44 "I ___ Little Prayer" (Warwick hit)
46 Title for Münchhausen
47 Gloomy atmosphere
49 Sgt. majors, e.g.
53 Hooked the trophy trout
56 *The King and I* location
57 De-creased
58 Golfer Trevino
59 Singer Seeger
60 Gravel ___ (*Dick Tracy* character)
61 Male cat or turkey
62 Wilma's hubby
63 Start of a Christmas hymn
64 They often get discounts: Abbr.

DOWN

1 Kelly who became a princess
2 Draw a bead on
3 Pig sniffer
4 Former leader of Iran
5 Made a doily
6 In a suggestive manner
7 "He's ___ goose"
8 Court precedent setter
9 Lit. compilation
10 Madonna's "Truth ___"
11 Flyer that once was sinking
12 Classroom projectile
13 Recipe amt.
21 Soviet prison camp
22 Seventh heaven
26 Roy Rogers's real last name
28 Providing a diversion, maybe
30 Rental ad abbr.
31 Corporeal
32 Common food preservative: Abbr.
34 Tarragon, e.g.
35 More on edge
36 Letters before an afterthought
37 Gummed up, with "with"
38 Sturm und ___
43 Added topsoil to
44 Angles
45 Even though
48 Go gaga over
50 Filly counterparts
51 It goes before "the other"
52 Appears (to be)
54 Start to byte
55 Nice notion
56 Tanning lotion letters

11 *A Day at the Office*

ACROSS

1 Waltzing lady of song
8 Right-angled triangle ratio
14 Unyielding in attitude
15 Orange crusher?
16 Office annoyance #1
18 Nile reptile
19 Tiber River capital
20 Omelette ingredient, for Caesar
21 Use a loom
23 Office annoyance #2
28 High: Prefix
31 Talk in church: Abbr.
32 Suffix with glob- or mod-
33 Adrienne Clarkson's husband
36 Punk's Pop
38 Dog-___ (worn, as an old book)
40 Office annoyance #3
43 Narrow mountain ridge
44 Performer's road trip
45 Song and dance?
46 Dept. head
47 Long-nosed jet, for short
49 May honourees
51 Office annoyance #4
54 Some daytime TV hosts
58 Info from the cockpit
59 Webzine
62 There's ___ in "team"
63 Office annoyance #5
67 Give a hand to
68 Wall-to-wall alternative
69 Woody and Tim
70 "See if I care!"

DOWN

1 Showy parrot
2 Give ___ of one's own medicine
3 ___ Bay Lightning
4 Mischievous child
5 Hardy mate
6 CBC radio show hosted by Sook-Yin Lee
7 "Up and ___!"
8 Coppertone stat.
9 19-Across's continent
10 More likely to be on the honour roll
11 ". . . partridge in ___ tree"
12 French sniffer
13 Three, in 19-Across
17 Sales agent, briefly
22 Porsche parker, perhaps
24 It's sought by a refugee
25 You might see this person in court
26 Northwest Territories weather station
27 Early Persians
29 Eye twitch
30 "This ___ see!"
33 Boggy place
34 Hair-tearer's cry
35 In ___ (unborn)
37 Gunk
39 Bring shame to
41 Put down new roots
42 Ranch addition
48 "___ Alive" (disco hit)
50 Robert Service's Sam, and others
52 Kathmandu's kingdom
53 Graphic beginning
55 Become used to
56 Online "round table"
57 Lightly burn
60 Degs. for curators
61 '70s do
63 *When Your Child Drives You Crazy* writer LeShan
64 Brooks or Blanc
65 Certain trains
66 Water of Lac Saint-Jean

12 *Summer's Landscape*

ACROSS

1 Evil in the extreme
8 Scot's cap
11 "Welcome" rug
14 Cocktail juice
15 "___ tree falls . . ."
16 Do 2+2
17 Gardening aids
19 Apt. ad info.
20 Be ___ (save the day)
21 *Star Wars* princess
22 Hit Lake Louise
23 Peel, as an apple
24 Gardening aids
27 Capital of Spain?
28 Cribbage marker
29 Counterparts to Houses
30 Skin cream brand
32 Cordwood measure
33 Gardening aids
37 "Where ___ keys?"
38 Butler in *Gone With the Wind*
39 Pond crosser
42 Start of the MGM motto
43 One of the five Ws
46 Gardening aid, if you have one
48 It may be for the birds
49 City council rep.
50 Big wheel at sea
51 Appalling
52 Kind of transmission: Abbr.
53 Gardening aids
55 Big shoebox letters
56 Go out ___ limb
57 Erode
58 Leary's drug
59 Second sight, for short
60 Affectionate with

DOWN

1 Tough spot
2 Waikiki welcomes
3 Spuds
4 Dean Martin's "That's ___"
5 Partnership for Peace grp.
6 "Is ___?" (Last Supper query)
7 It might give you a fat lip
8 Connections
9 Alpine chalet, often
10 Pas' mates
11 Telephone annoyance
12 Ones who look up to you
13 Blue Bomber scores
18 *Ben-Hur* author Wallace
22 Deal with, as a blackfly
24 Strauss of denim
25 Beginnings
26 Heading from Ottawa to NYC
28 Southwestern pine
30 Deadened
31 Farmer's field?: Abbr.
33 Distributes fair shares
34 Used the torch again
35 Car waxing cloths
36 Parsley, sage, or thyme
37 Chile neighbour: Abbr.
40 2004 Olympics city
41 Something you want to beat
43 "As if that ___ enough . . ."
44 Beneficiary of
45 Type of favourite
47 Nth: Abbr.
48 "___ Q" (1968 hit)
51 Labatt's label word
52 Poivre partner
53 Adversary
54 Barrister's field

■ BARBARA OLSON

13 *Excellent!*

ACROSS

1 Brit's bye-byes
6 Bog build-up
11 Party in Canada: Abbr.
14 "If ___ a Rich Man"
15 Surgical beam
16 Significant time
17 Excellent newcomer?
20 Estonia, once: Abbr.
21 Gymkhana gait
22 Parisian waterway
23 '50s dance, when doubled
24 Play place, to the south
26 Excellent tennis venue?
31 Innocent and guilty
32 Has a yen
33 Suffix meaning "foot"
36 Dr. Atkins no-no
37 Make happen
38 Service station job
39 Picnic pest
40 Kind of dog or pepper
41 Crow's claw
42 Excellent theft?
44 To the right: Fr.
47 Place ___ Beaux Arts
48 Harbour structures
49 Snail follower?
51 It's on in Québec

54 Excellent travel bag?
58 Narrow inlet
59 Classical guitarist Boyd
60 Urge on
61 "Yer darn tootin'"
62 Tugs
63 Bully's prey

DOWN

1 Reasons to wait?
2 Blows away
3 Nunavut is one: Abbr.
4 Rover's remark
5 Fumes
6 Lowest female voice
7 Stick it out
8 Conservative tax?
9 Bubbly prefix
10 Chalkboard accessories
11 Fair and right, in brief
12 Goodnight lady of song
13 More like Hubbard's
   cupboard
18 Stuff (in)
19 "Nifty!"
23 Surly one
24 Otolaryngologist's
   concern
25 Elephantine

26 Humane Soc. kin
27 Mongolia's capital ___
   Bator
28 Sassy
29 *Seinfeld* girl
30 Was able
33 Snivel
34 Jet black
35 Say no
37 Shoot the breeze
38 La Biche and Saint-Jean,
   for two
40 With chilly terseness
41 Ivy support
42 Al of *An Inconvenient
   Truth*
43 Sarah McLachlan tune
44 Copycat's behaviour
45 Whistle ___
46 Anchor's wrap-up
49 Monastery member
50 Santa ___ (hot winds)
51 They'll believe anything
52 Functions
53 Depend (on)
55 Spanish aunt
56 Charged atom
57 901 in Old Rome

14 *Start Groaning*

ACROSS

1 Read between the lines
6 "Cool," updated
10 Practise boxing
14 "___ break?"
15 Minimal amount
16 Get under control
17 Start of a quip
19 Lake bordering Ontario
20 Canola, for one
21 Tennis do-over
22 Big name in chips
23 Quip, part 2
27 Parcels out
30 Ant's construction
31 Product testing org. in Mississauga
34 John ___ (the Lone Ranger)
35 Pester to no end
37 Quip, part 3
40 "Keep your shirt on!"
41 Glasgow gal
42 Letters on a Cardinal's cap
43 Unit of loudness
44 Like thick soup
46 Quip, part 4
49 Toots
51 Seventh letter of the Greek alphabet
52 Fascist leader?
55 Malt drinks
56 End of quip
60 Bridge position
61 Not quite round
62 Slight taste
63 Too interested
64 Thesaurus wds.
65 Kind of fishing lure

DOWN

1 Enthusiastic about
2 Radar's favourite grape drink
3 Sense
4 One of eight Eng. kings
5 Lambaste
6 Michelangelo masterpiece
7 Question for Sherlock
8 One-time fill
9 Brits' thanks
10 Shorthand taker, for short
11 Finicky
12 Friendly femme
13 Rod attachment
18 Ottawa denizens, briefly
22 Its mecca is Mecca
23 Internet hookup device
24 American movie house
25 Winnie the Pooh's creator
26 Philosopher Zeno of ___
27 Ticat rivals
28 Resembled the Tower of Pisa
29 Sparkle
32 Looks at, in the Bible
33 Pretentious
35 *Cinderella* movie dog
36 Soviet prison camp
38 Kind of fit
39 Sufficient, in verse
44 ___ snag (got stuck)
45 Puts into law
47 In a snit
48 Ship "backbones"
49 Goldie of *Laugh-In*
50 Stick in the fridge?
52 Really small prefix
53 Hence, in logic
54 Rainbow, to some
56 ___ Lobos ("La Bamba" group)
57 Harvard's league
58 Kal ___ (Alpo alternative)
59 Clued in

■ BARBARA OLSON

15 *The Glass is Half Empty*

ACROSS

1 Huffy moods
6 Wooden box
11 Blood typing system
14 Drink at a coffee bar
15 ___ stock (carried, as merchandise)
16 ___ La Biche
17 Sought a reply
18 Versatile
20 Start of a quip
22 "That's ___ need!"
25 Short amount of time?
26 ___ even keel
27 More of the quip
31 Dissect a sentence
32 Rest atop
33 Meditator's moans
34 Military head: Abbr.
37 'Hood comrade
38 Crux
41 Work in America?
43 Rekindle
45 The quip continues
49 Le ___ (mine: Fr.)
50 Kilmer, and others
51 Right direction, often
52 End of the quip
56 Causes for alarms
57 Spell checker's flags
61 Rage
62 Spanish smooches
63 Prepare to drive
64 Apocryphal book: Abbr.
65 Monkey see, monkey do
66 Jean's *All in the Family* role

DOWN

1 Poet's wee
2 Refusals
3 "Gross!"
4 Miserable situation, slangily
5 "Smooth Operator" singer
6 Was "it"
7 Extremist
8 Biblical origin of woman
9 Wigwam
10 Tolkien tree beings
11 White rabbit, e.g.
12 Fragrant resin
13 Tar's place
19 "...followed by ___ shadow..." (Cat Stevens)
21 180° from NNW
22 Dog's breakfast, maybe
23 Actor Neeson
24 Env. stuffers
28 Compact Renault
29 ___-plunk!
30 Bed down in the henhouse
35 "May ___ of service?"
36 Opposite
38 Montreal-born rocker Aldo ___
39 Luau strings
40 Primo
41 ___ helping hand
42 House mover?
44 Like some '60s garb
45 Electricians, at times
46 Did as one was bid
47 Matte alternative
48 Egyptian cobra
49 Donny's singing sis
53 Isle of exile
54 Prez's right-hand man
55 Major finish
58 Potato prov.
59 Call at home
60 Round geom. solid

■ DAVE MACLEOD

16 *Prime Miniter*

ACROSS

1 Shutterbug's setting
6 Bit of merchandise
10 Accordingly
14 ___ *of Two Cities*
15 Lots and lots
16 It can be Near, Far or Middle
17 You run, bike and swim in these
19 Flies, to spiders
20 Prime Minister on a five
22 Tiny batteries
23 Earth Day subj.
24 Ashamed, for short
25 Banff four-footed forager
26 Roman gods
27 ___ Paese cheese
30 Dumbfounded
33 After-lunch sandwich
36 "Honest!"
38 Prime Minister on a fifty
41 *Ramayana* reader
42 Uzi predecessor
43 Copies
44 Japanese wraparound
45 Wrestler's surface
47 "Incidentally . . ."
49 Sis or bro
50 Minnow or worm
52 So-so grade

55 Prime Minister on a ten
59 Surrender, as territory
60 Food and water
61 To ___ (perfectly)
62 Start of Caesar's admonition
63 Ordered out?
64 Nudnik
65 Put one's foot down
66 Ladies' partners

DOWN

1 Islamic decree
2 Narrow groove
3 Coin toss option
4 Patron saint of Norway
5 "Diving" seabird
6 He hides in kids' books
7 Lagoon area
8 *The Road Taken* author Jaffe
9 Make certain
10 Not so hot?
11 Fabled also-ran
12 Computer jockey
13 Pig's digs
18 Wild Bill of the American west
21 Marie, par exemple
25 "Zounds!"
26 Nod off

27 Thing on a radar screen
28 ___ *Kleine Nachtmusik*
29 Crab order
30 What Seuss's Horton heard
31 Smooth-talking
32 Old Dodge
34 R and R part
35 *The Lord of the Rings* being
37 What a nod means
39 Curry flavouring
40 Where you likely are at -30°
46 Humiliates
48 Hard on the ears, for some
49 Piece of paper
50 Tend to the turkey
51 Be a brat
52 Chair maker, sometimes
53 Spanish national hero
54 Idyllic places
55 Ballet jump
56 Keats works
57 The tramp of *Lady and the Tramp*
58 Defence force of 1949: Abbr.
59 Salary limit

■ BARBARA OLSON

17 *Going Upscale*

ACROSS

1 Ring-bearing hobbit
6 Handheld computer, for short
9 "___ bleu!"
14 Spiked, as punch
15 Word of wonder
16 Ker-___ (kid's game)
17 Visitors to the National Gallery of Canada
19 Mark down prices
20 Corned beef cousin
21 Band's date
22 PEI clock setting
23 Wide-eyed
25 Certain sib
28 Unwed mother?
31 Haughty sort
32 Nursery shade, perhaps
33 TV-show segment
37 Kind of sprouts
39 Klingon clinger-on
40 "Dig in!"
41 The world's most prolific painter
42 Treater's announcement
43 "I'd hate to break up___"
44 Block, e.g.
46 Beanie baby brands
47 "May I help you?"
48 Reason for sneezin'

49 Roman's 205
52 "Nein" contradictions
53 Strait of Georgia island
58 Pig's kin
61 David Beckham's first chauffeur?
62 Get ___ of (contact)
63 Hawaiian dish
64 Retail giant
65 Page of music?
66 Sum up?
67 Complex dwelling

DOWN

1 Tent door
2 ___ avis (strange bird)
3 Turkey dinner mos.
4 BC's Fraser Valley city
5 Smells, to the south
6 Robert Service output
7 Wilde's *The Picture of ___ Gray*
8 Sounds of relief
9 Bit of parsley
10 Words with shake or break
11 Cry on the set
12 Matter of life
13 Heart reading: Abbr.
18 Wine vessel
21 Wine vessel

24 Ken Dryden, once
25 Like old movies
26 Negative notoriety
27 Footwear for Kurt Browning
28 What workers take home
29 Prepare to revolt
30 Some family reunion attendees
31 Show to the door
32 El ___, Texas
34 Trick-taking game with 32 cards
35 Gives the nod
36 Sock hop successors
38 Army posts, often: Abbr.
45 Parent's parting words
48 ___ Gras (New Orleans festival)
49 *Air Farce* airer
50 Get louder, in mus.
51 Small, olive-green bird
52 Drop like a hot potato
54 Hydrochloric ___
55 Saudi Arabia neighbour
56 Lady's man
57 Kid's retort to a skeptic
58 Bug on the phone?
59 "I've got it!"
60 Ante's place
61 Place to sweat it out

18 *Pour a Cold One*

ACROSS

1 Avalanche chute bushes
7 Heavenly bodies
11 Not prov.
14 Hardy partner
15 Baseball schedule adjustment
17 Going up, in a way
18 Fort exit for troops
19 Ingredient #1
20 It may get thrown for a loss
22 Ingredient #2
23 Native: Suffix
24 Thong feature
27 Bras ___ Lakes, Cape Breton
28 Alley cat
30 Broken, as a wild horse
32 Genes material
34 Happy days
36 Used cars?
37 Y, pluralized
38 Instruction #1
43 Norse god of war
44 *Star Trek* helmsman
45 Actress Ullmann
46 Where the buoys and gulls are
47 Government investment, familiarly
49 Path's beginning?

53 Early year in Nero's reign
55 Play the vamp
57 K-O span
58 Ingredient #3
60 Measure of resistance
61 Ingredient #4
62 Black cat, maybe
65 Composer Shostakovich
67 Email forerunner
68 Extremely popular
69 They, in Baie Comeau
70 Beget
71 Place for an ace

DOWN

1 Los ___ (where the first atomic bomb was developed)
2 Big name in this puzzle's theme
3 More boring
4 Part of Q.E.D.
5 ___-de-chaussée (ground floor)
6 Winter toys
7 Instruction #2
8 Explorer of the Canadian Arctic
9 Lobsterfest necessity
10 Hank of Canadian country music
11 Account for

12 Means of computer networking
13 Howl : wolf :: bell : ___
16 Couple of anything
21 Hairy TV cousin
24 Clerk, at times
25 Latin love
26 Gas or brake, e.g.
29 It borders It.
31 Downward slide
33 Tree with straight-grained wood
35 Ticket proof
38 Petrol amts.
39 Aiming height
40 Life's problems
41 Polar bear's transport
42 Lacto-___ vegetarian
48 Response from a doofus
50 Dress
51 Famed LA comedy club, with "The"
52 Like some training
54 Cruise stopover
56 Precinct heads: Abbr.
58 Sasquatch cousin
59 Threads
61 Early Hudson's Bay Company quest
63 Hosp. scan
64 Musical discernment
66 Gibson of *Mad Max*

19 *Hurry Up and Wait*

ACROSS

1 Invitation request
8 Merriment
14 Oscar Wilde title word
15 Open markets
16 "Timely" observation, part 1
18 Like a rat to a gnat, say
19 Contradicts
20 *The Crying Game* actor Stephen
23 ___ *for Alibi* (Sue Grafton)
24 Study of plants: Abbr.
27 Part 2 of the observation
33 PC connection
34 ___ buco (veal dish)
35 Ending for a lover
36 Decked out
38 Fought tooth and nail
40 Leaf's pore
41 Cubs' slugger Sammy
42 Mama's boys
43 Part 3 of the observation
47 Barrett of Pink Floyd
48 Caesarian 56
49 Leaves for a fortune teller
50 Got by
53 Keeper of *North of 60*
57 End of the observation
61 Grave event
62 Is enamoured by
63 Rock's ___ Dan
64 Wise (up)

DOWN

1 Its cap. is Amsterdam
2 Pearl Harbor's island
3 Actor Peck, to his pals
4 Doctor's trainee
5 Not agin
6 Classical grp. in Ontario
7 Rip-off at a concert?
8 Pertaining to France
9 Favouring the young
10 "How much do ___ you?"
11 Goddess of discord
12 Make lace
13 Lazy assent
17 Bingo kin
21 Director of *Ararat*
22 Church recess
24 Carefree
25 Slicker
26 Lethal injector
27 Novice trumpeter's sounds
28 Resembling soil, in colour or smell
29 Encroachment
30 TSX figure
31 Latest report
32 Captor's cry
37 Qty.
38 Ground breaker
39 NHL stat.
41 Nasty, as a remark
44 What a butter-upper might call you
45 Too much so
46 Wonderland character
50 Maned mom
51 ". . . blackbirds baked in ___"
52 Thanksgiving mos.
54 Superlative suffix
55 Casual evening
56 Scads
57 Cable-TV channel
58 "Damn spot" preceder
59 "___ Canadian!" (Molson slogan)
60 Alias

20 *Let's Rock*

ACROSS

1. Nova Scotia native: Var.
7. Kind of door lock
15. Crazy Horse's Sioux tribe
16. Abyssinia now
17. Slimy Vancouver band?
19. ___-disant (self-styled)
20. Boxes up
21. Nerd
25. Ex-queen of Jordan
27. Really dry
28. They pitch things on TVs
30. Arises (from)
33. Sound after a puncture
34. "Ach du ___!"
36. Formal wear
38. Sad but cool Kingston band, with "The"?
42. Further down
43. Kind of roll
45. German okays
48. Puff up
50. Thing with a tripwire
51. Jocks: Abbr.
53. Short time span, shortly
55. Word with farm or muffin
56. Stiff drinks
59. Make a collar
61. Toronto band of Adamites?
67. Type of forecast
68. Unhealthy atmosphere
69. Asking for more *Time*
70. "You couldn't have waited?"

DOWN

1. Stylish
2. "Can ___ now?"
3. Gulager of *The Virginian*
4. 'Zine
5. Word of woe
6. Camera name
7. RCMP rank
8. Gossamer
9. "Two owls and ___ . . .": Lear
10. Platter
11. Gauchos' weapons
12. Literary works
13. Feline hybrids
14. Thé cups
18. "Madre de ___ !"
21. Guy's girl
22. Cut and paste, e.g.
23. Part of ER: Abbr.
24. Skewered item
26. Natives for whom a capital is named
29. Israeli desert
31. Take advantage of, in a way
32. ___ a fox
35. Lunar valley
37. Climbs, as a pole
39. Type of cap with a tail
40. The wolf ___ the door
41. A bean is named for its capital
44. Hockey player Kelly
45. Talk too much
46. Vanish without ___
47. Ariel of Israel
49. Be inclined (to)
52. Brouhaha
54. Sedates
57. Aplenty, once
58. Branches, in botany
60. Scott of sitcoms
62. Heart readout: Abbr.
63. Start of a Marx title
64. Bar opener?
65. Funnyman Philips
66. Word before Jose or Juan

■ DAVE MACLEOD

21 *Let's Roll*

ACROSS

1 Fish tanks
8 One peeking through a keyhole
13 SMALL WILD HORSE
14 Like many Greek statues
17 Kind of novel
18 City northeast of Thunder Bay
19 Thousand Island alternative
20 Goddess: Lat.
21 "I'll take that as ___"
22 Beaver feature
23 Cotillion girl, for short
25 One of Whitman's bloomers
27 Communication without talking: Abbr.
28 Sea World star
30 Prince Valiant's wife
31 Lead-in to nose or hair
32 Pound sound
34 Part of Q,E,D,
35 Places to find the answers to the capitalized clues
38 Rope tow relative
40 Bambi's aunt
41 Gilbert and Sullivan princess
42 Sewing machine inventor Howe

44 Common motor design
46 ___ Dhabi
49 Decaf brand
50 Want ad inits.
51 In a bit, to the Bard
52 Gem wt.
53 ___-de-lance (viper)
55 Kneels, perhaps
58 Annuls, as a bylaw
60 Go over again
61 Ladd role in *Saskatchewan* (1954)
62 PETALS, COLLECTIVELY
63 Takes a stab at
64 Israeli parliament

DOWN

1 Hindu beverage of immortality
2 Sales targets
3 Canada Post equiv. to the south
4 In any way
5 Indian princess
6 Ancient Andean
7 It may be hidden
8 Poet Carl
9 ___-dieu (kneeling platform)
10 ANIMAL WITH LYRE-SHAPED HORNS

11 Whitney or Wallach
12 They party hearty
15 MOZART PIECE
16 High-country winter transport
24 Come (from)
26 "___ Song Go Out of My Heart" (Ellington)
28 Assad's land: Abbr.
29 Cod kin
31 Ehud of Israel
33 Smart-alecky
35 Artist's bucket
36 Cosecants, to sines
37 Laudatory lines
38 Spanish treasure
39 SPORTS JACKET
43 KENYAN ADVENTURE
45 Friend of Hamlet
46 Chronicles
47 Enclose, with "up"
48 Oust
51 Bubbly chocolates
54 Sommer of cinema
56 College on the Thames
57 Drummondville dad
59 Where It. is

46

22 *Jumbled Words*

ACROSS

1 Shared the puck
7 Certain trains
10 Aquarium growth
14 Worrier's woes
15 Call at home?
16 Needing a mend
17 ASTRONOMER, jumbled up
19 Opposed to, yokel-style
20 Bar figure: Abbr.
21 Cuts corners, say
23 SLOT MACHINES, jumbled up
26 Ness's pursuit
29 Show for Aykroyd, once: Abbr.
30 DORMITORY, jumbled up
34 Prenuptial parties
38 Swear words?
39 Revenue Canada checkup
41 Inst. manual heading
42 Explorer ___ da Gama
45 ANIMOSITY, jumbled up
48 Form ender
50 Not for family viewing
51 PRESBYTERIAN, jumbled up
57 Way over one's head
58 Measure of warmth: Abbr.
61 Shirk work, with "off"
62 GEORGE BUSH, jumbled up
66 Norwegian saint
67 Prefix meaning "egg"
68 "City of Parks" in BC's Fraser Valley
69 Felines, to Tweety
70 Hump day: Abbr.
71 Entrees at Hy's

DOWN

1 Fast cat
2 Scads
3 Sir John A. Macdonald, for one
4 Red Chamber mem.
5 Staller's syllables
6 Summer setting: Abbr.
7 Pink shade
8 New: Sp.
9 Workaholic's woe
10 Askew
11 Use a password
12 Fairy-tale brother
13 Calendrier span
18 Kind of 59-Down
22 RR stops
23 Guest bed, maybe
24 ___ day now
25 Will be, in a Doris Day song
26 404, in Old Rome
27 Verdi opera (1871)
28 Good points
31 Péquiste vote
32 Takes too much, quickly
33 Simmer setting: Abbr.
35 Have ___ (blow one's stack)
36 Terminal site
37 8.23 m^2
40 Belinda Stronach, formerly
43 What to make of old jeans
44 Hodgepodge
46 "You ___ here"
47 Scratch the surface, say
49 "Amen!"
51 Archie Bunker, for one
52 ___ Gay (WW II plane)
53 Short-tailed weasel
54 Tick off
55 Make another offer
56 Kwik-E-Mart owner
58 Bred partner
59 See 18-Down
60 Driver's 180s
63 It became 6% on July 1, 2006
64 Stand-in at school
65 Miracle-___ (garden brand)

23 What's Missing, Eh?

ACROSS

1 R-V interior?
4 Loosens
11 *Brokeback Mountain* director Lee
14 Army bed
15 Falls between two countries?
16 Chatroom chuckle
17 In the manner of
18 Shrugs off
19 La-la lead-in
20 Tell the poison ivy story again?
22 Some Blue Bombers: Abbr.
23 Rib donor
24 Case studier: Abbr.
25 Dummy's replies
26 Mackerel kin
30 It happens in the east
32 Woody's boy
34 Moves slowly and carefully
35 Conductor Zubin riding a subway?
40 Pago Pago locale
41 Bit of bird food
42 It's named for a princess
45 Printer's dash
50 One third of the Golden Triangle
51 Solo of *Star Wars*
53 Internet auctioneer
54 Latin for "strength"
55 Surfers' gleeful cry?
59 Nincompoop
60 Standing for
61 Mountain pass
62 Whiz start
63 Two-time Emmy winner Fabray
64 Mentalist Geller
65 Formula One curve
66 Occupy completely
67 Kind of transmission: Abbr.

DOWN

1 Egyptian beetle
2 "Holy ___!"
3 Marie Osmond, for one
4 Les États- ___
5 Almost, in poems
6 Superman's "other" girlfriend Lang
7 Greek marketplace
8 Gem measures
9 1970s song subtitled "Touch the Wind"
10 Merit badge holder
11 He's no egoist
12 Arm of the Atlantic
13 They're for drinking or seeing
21 French friend
25 Pharmacist's weight
27 Steppes settler: Var.
28 "... boy___ girl?"
29 ___-mo
31 More than wants
33 Walk-___ (minor parts)
35 La Salle lethargies
36 Raises, as type
37 Removes weeds
38 Place for swingers
39 Haw's partner
40 Sunken ship recovery
43 Like the ruins at Luxor and Karnak
44 Making spa sounds
46 Bench in a church
47 Summer in the East
48 Romp
49 Blinker
52 US consumer advocate Ralph
55 Wind down
56 Godfather Corleone
57 Tolkien creatures
58 Seemingly forever

■ BARBARA OLSON

24 *Just for the L of It*

ACROSS

1 *The World at Six* wrap-up
6 Browning's "___ Lippo Lippi"
9 Donald's ex
14 Draw at Tim Hortons
15 Land of the Ural Mtns.
16 Went to the polls
17 Prenatal learning session?
19 Curmudgeon's countenance
20 Diver's milieu
22 Prefix meaning "high"
23 It may be left of centre?
26 Marine creature that eats everything in its sight?
28 Undercover partner
31 Hebrew alphabet ender
32 DOS part: Abbr.
33 Bonspieler's need
34 There's a moral to his stories
36 Strategic duo?
41 Nova Scotia town
42 Hot Wheels sound, to a tike
44 Chest muscle, for short
47 "Don't ___" ("Never mind")
48 Cover up at a duel
50 Reason to carry a spare?

53 ___ populi
54 *Leave ___ Beaver*
55 Mistakenly
58 J.D. Salinger's *Franny and ___*
60 Movie about Oscar Madison?
64 Mr. Dressup, off air
65 The whole shootin' match
66 Where Don McLean drove his Chevy
67 Mottled horses
68 Word div.
69 ___ bin Laden

DOWN

1 Factor in computing capacity: Abbr.
2 Big time
3 URL ender
4 Make ___ dash for it
5 Show anxiety
6 Blender setting
7 Actress Rene of *Ransom*
8 Said 59-Down
9 ICU life lines
10 List for an ESL student
11 Island strings
12 Under-the-tree item
13 Improv bits
18 For fear that

21 Shocked breathless
23 Shoreline recession
24 Crime committer, in cop talk
25 "Rebel Yell" singer Billy
27 Support Darwin, in a way
29 Not worth debating
30 Vehicle for landing troops
34 Year, to Juan
35 Chute opener
37 Food served at a bar
38 Bill Clinton's state
39 Bad kid's penance
40 Arty New York area
43 Tex-___
44 Viagra maker
45 Corrida gorer
46 ___ *Hot Tin Roof* (Tennessee Williams)
48 How users get down?
49 Dhaliwal or Gray
51 Wheel alignment adjustment
52 "Promiscuous Girl" girl
56 Capital on a fjord
57 Posties' paths: Abbr.
59 No alternative
61 Lab eggs
62 Dream state, briefly
63 Thumbs-up on the Hill

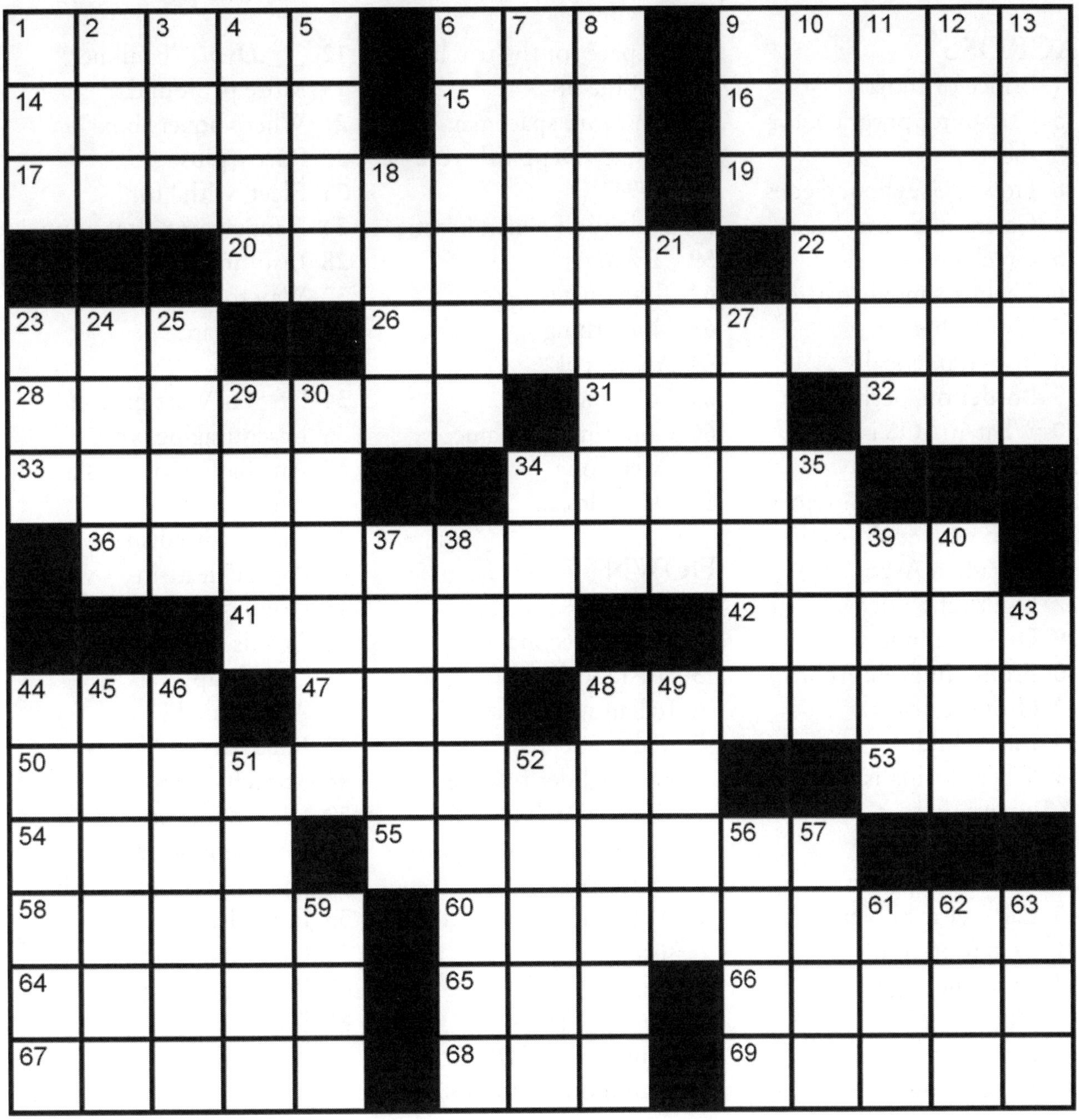

25 *Number Please*

ACROSS

1 Prince of India
5 Computer program, for short
8 How a Greyhound goes
14 Galena and cinnabar
15 Greek cross
16 Thelma's movie partner
17 Fly catcher
18 Planet, poetically
19 Border on, perhaps
20 What an SOS is
23 Acorn, eventually
25 "No, you're not" retort
26 John who explored the Canadian Arctic
27 Light refractor
29 Do something
30 From Nineveh: Abbr.
32 Groupie, usually
33 Like a fiddle
34 Where losing is intentional
35 Gang kingpins
39 Homer's outburst
40 Early year in Nero's reign
41 1998 toon film
44 Someone ___ fault
47 Hula hoop?
48 January, in Juárez
49 Anonymous John
50 Prepare for the trip home
52 Gobble up
53 *Toy Story* spaceman
57 Johnny Depp title role (1994)
58 Hideous Tolkien beastie
59 "By Jove!"
62 Take on again
63 Not a thing
64 Aussie pal
65 Food merchant
66 Computer filename extension
67 Dance lesson

DOWN

1 CD- ___
2 Jackie's second
3 Sea-Doo user
4 Italian wine centre
5 Make amends
6 Hang-glider relative
7 Where you'll hear the beginning of 20-, 35- or 53-Across
8 Welcome sight in the spring
9 Take ___ pick
10 He was "The Babe"
11 Four-time NHL champions in the 1980s
12 ___ *Dying* (Faulkner)
13 More profound
21 Where boxers box
22 Portly plus
23 Elect, with "for"
24 It may come after you
28 Insulting, as a remark
30 Way to go
31 It's a wrap
33 E-I filler
34 US Star Wars project
36 Discouraging words
37 Amelia Earhart was a famous one
38 Views with disdain
42 "La-la" lead-in
43 Comics lightning sound
44 Tennis great Stefan
45 "Speak up!"
46 "Oh yeah?!"
47 Race part
48 Scratch (out)
50 Clause add-on
51 Repeating series
54 Paleo- or Meso- finish
55 Folktales
56 Gets ready to fire
60 Put away the groceries
61 Slangy assent

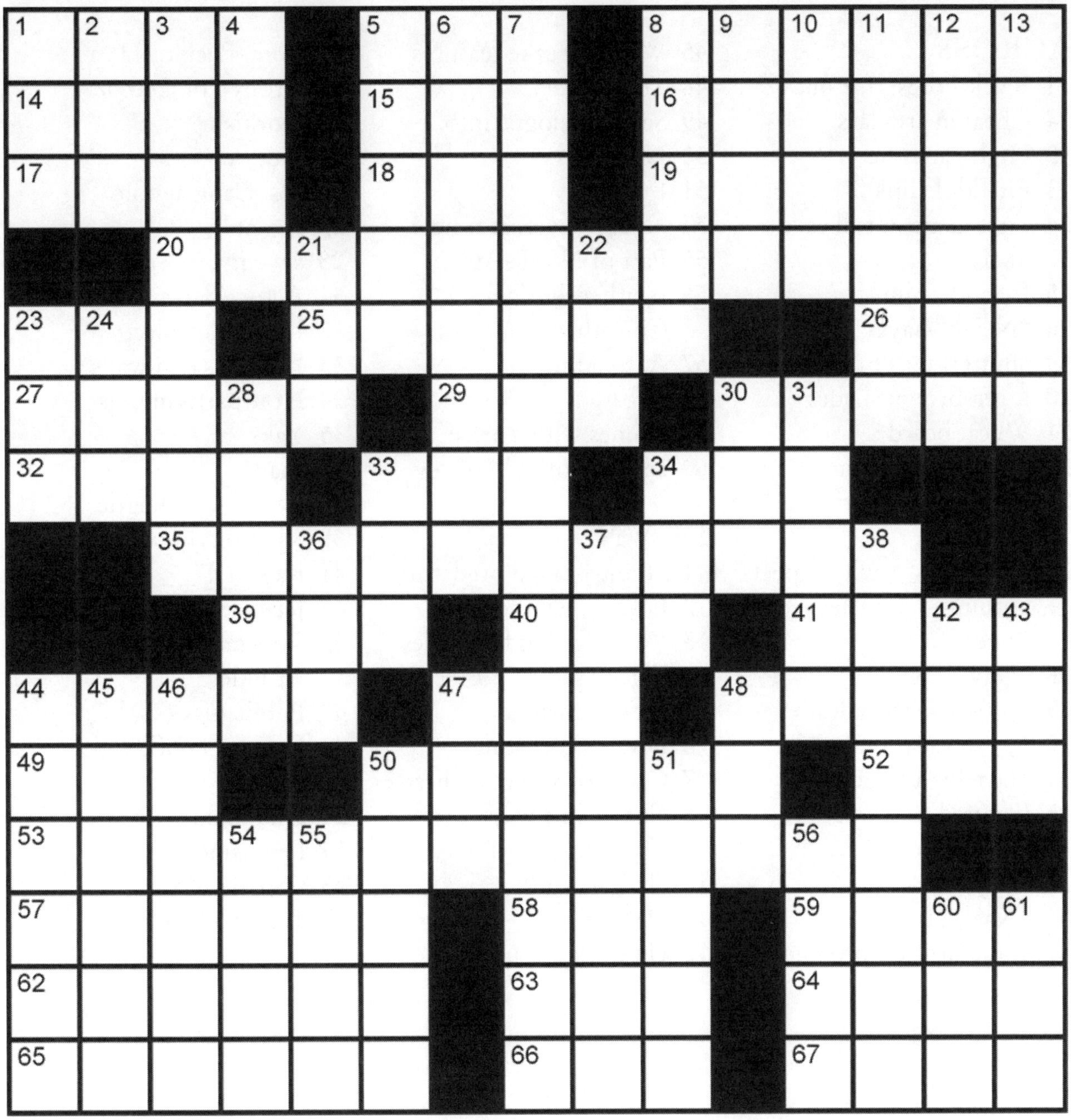

26 *Just Say Nay, or Nae, or . . .*

ACROSS

1 Black Forest, for one
4 Cheat in art class
9 High hairstyle
13 Fit-fiddle link
14 First name in roll call, likely
15 Ireland's Sinn ___
16 "Neigh"-sayer
19 Shutterbug's brand
20 Light brown shades
21 Wheat beard
23 Opposite of stern
24 Radium Hot Springs emission
25 "Blessed ___ who expects nothing . . .": Alexander Pope
26 "Nay"-sayer
29 ___ worse than death
30 "___ a vacation"
31 Have high hopes
35 Knotted, as a tree
36 ___ behold
37 Stray's lack
40 "Nae"-sayer
44 Some Molson products
45 Wedding cake features
46 Top banana
49 Sears catalogue info.
50 Not poetry
51 Bungle
52 "Nez"-sayer, at times?
55 Part of NWT: Abbr.
56 Neither Doric nor Corinthian
57 A, to Aline
58 Leg up
59 Comes with a price
60 Lindsay of old hockey

DOWN

1 Hook-beaked predators
2 Give ___ in the arm
3 Young girl in fairy tales
4 Tiger's place, in Esso ads
5 Bit of sunshine
6 Diva's short song
7 Cause of a swollen head?
8 Cut in, in a way
9 Sky lights, maybe
10 Slash in km/h
11 Major flop
12 Unicycle feature
17 Tom, Dick or Harry
18 Cronyn of *Cocoon*
22 Dorkish
24 Not out
25 Ms. Campagnolo
27 Avant-___
28 Twenty, in Trois-Rivières
31 Actor Alan and family
32 Life companion
33 Like '70s den walls
34 Non-partisan pols.
35 Yaks
37 Inane
38 Retort to a skeptic
39 Soup serving dishes
41 Raison d'___
42 Jet-black
43 Winetaster's nose-wrinkler
47 Public fuss
48 Destroy confidential papers
50 Untainted
51 Pen names
53 Grp. or assn.
54 Take a load off

■ DAVE MACLEOD

27 *Nips at Noon*

ACROSS
1 Fi lead-in
4 Modern way to transfer docs.
7 ___ *Park* (2001 whodunit)
14 Foothills town west of Calgary
16 Asthmatic's relief giver
17 Stop sign shape
18 *Blondie* mailman Mr. ___
19 Start of a question from W.C. Fields
21 Give for a while
22 Singer LaBelle
23 Saturated with
27 *Biography* airer
31 Put the kibosh on
32 Animation collectible
33 More of the question
40 Newfoundland catch, once
41 Kitchen gizmo
42 Oktoberfest vessel
45 Derringers, e.g.
49 ___ spell on
51 "I ___ bad moon . . ."
52 End of the question
57 Pedicurist's target

58 "Good job!"
59 New Orleans pirate Jean
60 Film ender, usually
61 Trite
62 Chunk of green
63 Whole bunch

DOWN
1 Expresses dissatisfaction
2 Mark of prestige
3 Chant
4 Gets blurry, with "up"
5 Harness race pace
6 Cambodia's Phnom ___
7 Lebanese poet Kahlil
8 ___ a time (singly)
9 Volcanic peak of the Cascades
10 British car dashboard
11 Stew, or the pot it's stewed in
12 Country dance
13 Like Chianti
15 Winless racehorses
20 Skin-related
24 Orchestra or casino section
25 "Outside" prefix

26 Erase, on a comp.
28 Sgt. or cpl.
29 German title start
30 Banff beast
33 Loos
34 In, for now
35 Praiseful poem
36 ___ Maria
37 Stomach acid, symbolically
38 Jellied delicacy
39 Froze, as a computer
43 Representative in style or appearance
44 "Broadway Joe" of Super Bowl III
45 Done up, as hair
46 Make sure the water's safe
47 Have it in mind
48 Most wise
50 Clobber, biblically
52 Stable newborn
53 Mortgage option, briefly
54 Reunion attendees, informally
55 Robert De ___
56 Sent a duplicate, for short
57 RN's specialty

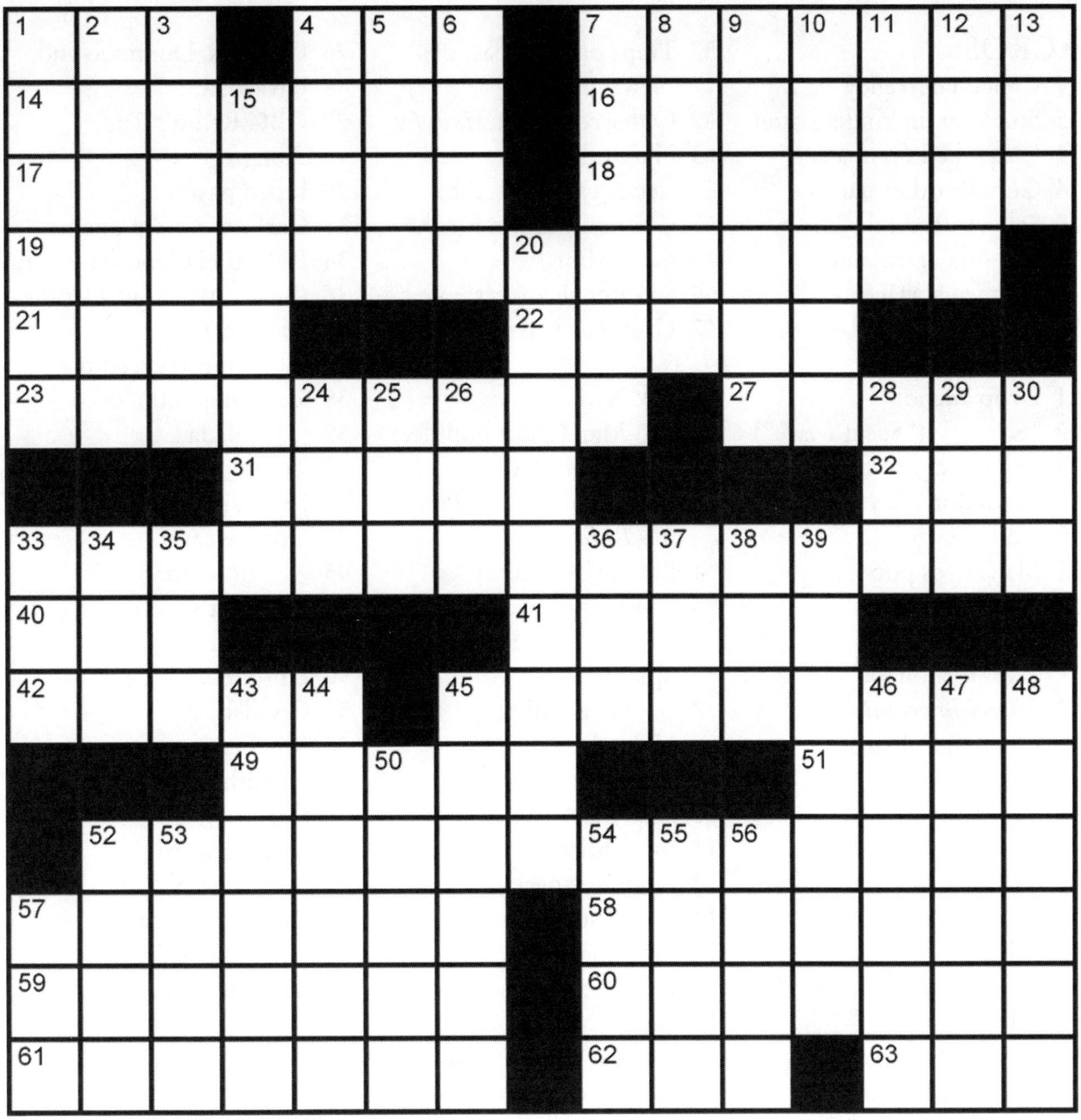

28 *Mixed Messages*

ACROSS

1 Cancún currency
5 Stuck on, in kindergarten
11 It's picked up in a bar
14 Cupid's other name
15 Self-centred one
16 Bed-In participant
17 Kitchen surfaces
19 Hang ___ thread
20 "Sit!"
21 Drop anchor
22 "So, ___" ("See if I care")
24 Pay to get out of jail
28 "You don't say!"
30 Adds oxygen
31 Make eyes pop
32 Number (of)
35 Keeps going, after giving it some thought
40 *The Homecoming* playwright Harold
41 Roman poet
43 Superlatively silly
47 Peaceful
49 Random test for quality control
52 Wild
53 "Ver-r-r-y interesting!" Johnson
54 Equally talented
56 Orange Muppet
57 Traps off the coast of Newfoundland
62 Older cousin of *Mad TV*
63 Harem honcho
64 Letter carriers? Abbr.
65 Communication for the deaf: Abbr.
66 Sweater shrinkers, maybe
67 Urquhart Castle's loch

DOWN

1 ___-Man (ghost gobbler)
2 Comedian Philips
3 Like some cars on *Pimp My Ride*
4 Bauble or bead
5 Cheat at hide-and-seek
6 "Get ___!" ("Smarten up!")
7 ___ voce (quietly)
8 Mañuel's uncle
9 Second sight, initially
10 Shaky times at AA
11 In addition
12 Nobody special
13 Directors sit on them
18 Sap's place
21 Deg. for a pitcher?
22 Fam. sibling
23 Golden rule preposition
25 Stir-fry direction
26 Carreras, Domingo and Pavarotti
27 CBC Radio's *The ___ Tonight*
29 Filled pastry
33 Carlo or Cristo opener
34 Rideau Hall locale: Abbr.
36 On ___ (without a contract)
37 Unwrapped greedily
38 Too long in the oven
39 ___ colada
42 Tierra ___ Fuego
43 Eva's sister of film
44 Cook wear?
45 ___ motel (tryst site)
46 Resident's suffix
48 ___ effort
50 Untouchables, e.g.
51 Coolish sun
55 Mil. bigwigs
57 Something to take on a trip?
58 Sharing word
59 Journalist Nellie
60 Sports-bar fixtures
61 Sound made by a defensive cat

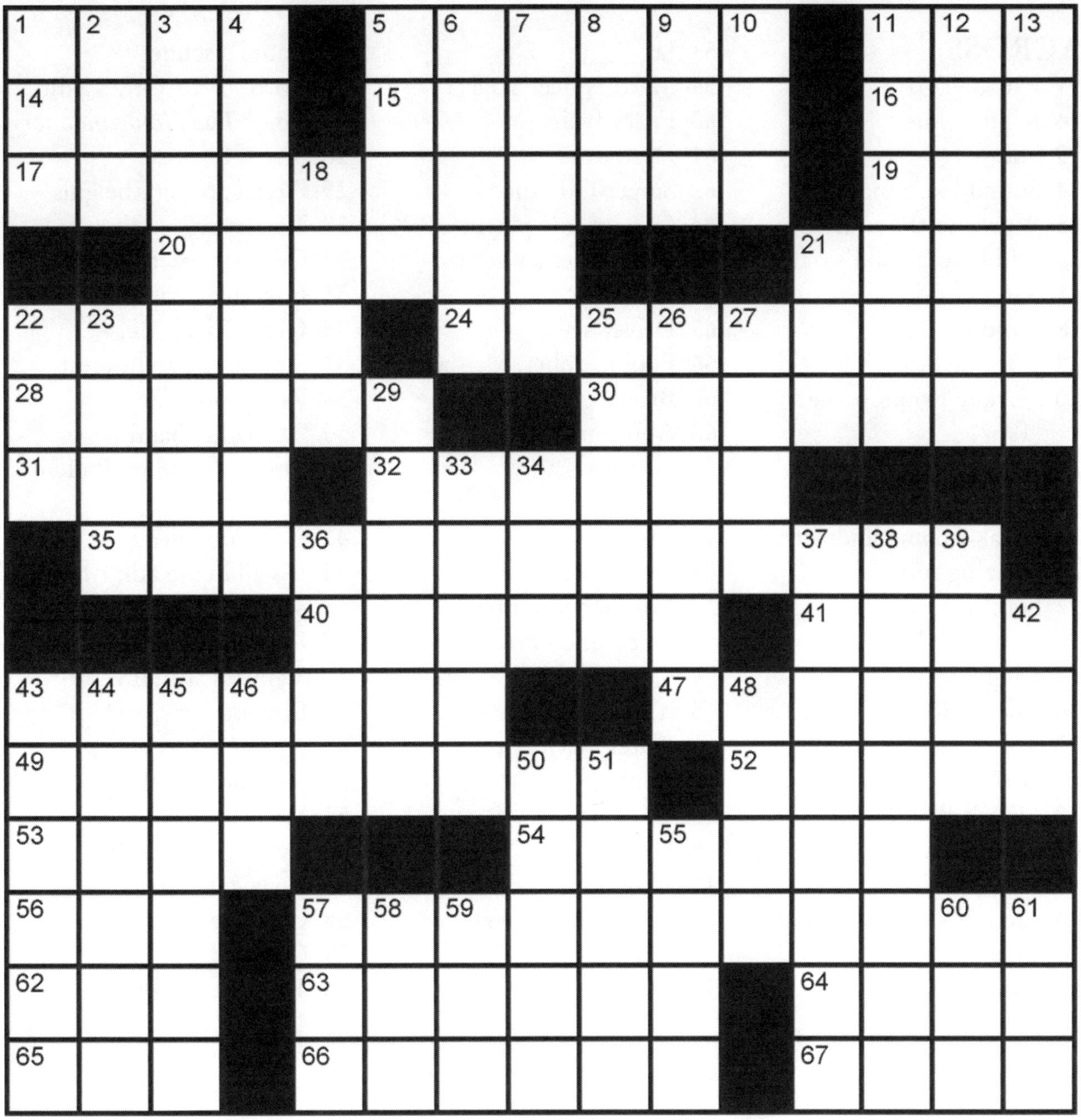

29 *Misguided Youth*

ACROSS

1 Part of TGIF
4 Kind of nut
9 Shrew
14 Sound like a pigeon
15 Words to the audience
16 Old MacDonald's refrain
17 Kind of tide
18 Jargon
19 Burning desire?
20 Mickey Rooney role (1957)
23 *A Death in the Family* author
24 Break a commandment
25 Grazing spot
27 Status of Zeus and Jupiter
31 Drop off
34 Ring response
36 Like xenon and neon
37 Kris Kristofferson role (1973)
40 CBer's B
42 Renter's notice
43 Nearby Maple Leaf rival
46 *West Side Story* hit song
50 Query
51 'Dozer name
53 Jai ___
54 Martin Sheen role (1974)
60 Furry fruit
61 Dead duck
62 Singer DiFranco
63 Certain role player
64 Shout after some arm-twisting
65 Driver's aid
66 Pool member, for short
67 Bruins great Cam
68 Abbr. missing from modern maps

DOWN

1 Sprain application
2 Trinidad's companion
3 Cried uncontrollably
4 ___-baked (unrealistic)
5 It's east of the Urals
6 Battery element
7 Rims
8 Mr. Brezhnev
9 Mend
10 What fops put on
11 Found the answer
12 Sony rival
13 Hither's partner
21 Rabbi's school
22 Toronto-to-Ottawa dir.
26 Ed of *The Honeymooners*
28 Serf
29 Green around the gills
30 Tire layer
32 Compare, with "to"
33 First in a series
35 Giant Giant Mel
37 Standard loan interest
38 Really popular
39 "Xanadu" band
40 Org. inspired by Baden-Powell
41 Aretha spelled it
44 It's all in the fall: Abbr.
45 Sci-fi zapper
47 Is a bad winner
48 Stainless steel inventor Elwood
49 Neater
52 Steakhouse offering
55 MBA's course
56 By way of, briefly
57 Fairy-tale starter
58 Get loud
59 Glenn of The Eagles
60 The ___, Manitoba

■ BARBARA OLSON

30 *Now Here's a Switch*

ACROSS

1 Masked scavenger, for short
5 "Nuke," maybe
11 Frowned-on flavour enhancer
14 Taurus or Aries
15 Lots
16 Flock female
17 Expert brewer of dark beer?
19 Sn, to a chemist
20 "Heavens ___!"
21 Prefix meaning "equal"
22 Old West novelist Grey
23 Characteristic of Lévesque?
25 Develop, as events
27 Walks along a Mideast saltwater lake?
30 Don't waste
31 Police informers, slangily
32 Had been
35 Twice, musically
36 Older monitor component: Abbr.
37 Common Latin ending?
41 Classroom trainees, for short
44 Hypnotist's trade?
48 Limp and lifeless
49 Literary laments
51 TV's 86 and 99: Abbr.
52 This partner
54 ___-biter (toddler)
55 LI, doubled
56 Angry jeweller's projectile?
58 Surfer's destination
59 Driver's flagpole
60 Newsy bit
61 Carpet thickness
62 Doesn't relish
63 Diddly-squat

DOWN

1 Mexican homes
2 Win on eBay
3 Peter of *The Stunt Man* (1980)
4 It's new in Québec
5 Tach reading
6 Go by, as time
7 "For ___ jolly good fellow . . ."
8 Puts one's faith in
9 Eroded
10 Norse god of strife
11 Copper-tasting, say, as water
12 Pig-in-a-poke peddler
13 Kind of pool
18 Minds, with "to"
22 Biol. branch
24 Half of a fly?
26 Big do
28 Like David Suzuki
29 Retired jet, for short
32 *Scream* director Craven
33 Proud remark to a daugher
34 How some cover girls are clad
35 Commercial flyer?
38 "___ Tu" (1974 hit)
39 President pro ___
40 Transistor electrode
41 Former phone company BC ___
42 Fields
43 Logs on
45 Start to steam
46 Former Soviet leader Khrushchev
47 Got firm
50 "Doesn't it ___ little odd?"
51 Bra size
53 Sarah McLachlan tune
56 Down
57 They, to Théo

■ DAVE MACLEOD

31 *Let It Snow!*

ACROSS

 1 Bavarian capital
 7 Shrinking Asian sea
11 Building add-on
14 Maroon, like Robinson Crusoe
15 Have ___ in the matter
16 As well
17 With 59-Across, first line of the puzzle's title song
20 Young golf phenom Michelle
21 They're put on for show
22 You hope they'll meet
23 Goes like Donovan Bailey
25 Go- ___ (kid's race car)
28 With 46-Across, second line of the song
33 Insomniac's need
36 Mythical medieval beasts
37 Source of many drafts
38 Often ___ (half the time)
40 Hockey's Bobby
41 About to miss a deadline, perhaps
44 Argon and neon
46 See 28-Across
49 Potter's oven
50 Handy reference
54 Prefix with European
57 World War II alliance
58 Smelter input

59 See 17-Across
64 Ottoman officer
65 Haircut or rug type
66 Backus role on *Gilligan's Island*
67 Investigator's question
68 Bubbly chocolate bar
69 Prairie homes: Var.

DOWN

 1 Pet sounds
 2 Nerdy
 3 US gunpowder component
 4 "Sort of" suffix
 5 Win all the awards, so to speak
 6 Legendary hockey announcer Foster
 7 Small batts.
 8 Q-U queue
 9 Massage reaction
10 Caustic solution
11 Henry VI founded it
12 Like Hawaiian shirts
13 Builders' sites
18 Once, once
19 Fashionably old-fashioned
24 "May ___ excused?"
25 Lotto-like game
26 Something to have or throw

27 Guitarist Ocasek of The Cars
29 Sneaking suspicion
30 Cupid, to Greeks
31 Memo phrase
32 Lat. and Lith., once
33 Frequents Banff or Whistler
34 Jokester Jay
35 "My stars!"
38 Blue dye
39 Omen
42 Type of tea
43 "Thrilla in Manila" victor
44 Detective, in old slang
45 Carte or mode lead-in
47 Curbside waiter
48 Alternative to fight
51 Pro bono lawyers work for this
52 As ___ (generally)
53 You use grey ones when solving crosswords
54 "___ Her Standing There" (Beatles)
55 Almost, in poems
56 WW II turning point
57 Toronto gridder
60 "This ___ test"
61 Any ship, for short
62 Remote
63 Community designation: Abbr.

32 *Where R You?*

ACROSS

1 Gift ___
6 In favour of
9 Borden's bill, slangily
14 Natural bath sponge
15 ___ creek without . . .
16 Pong creator
17 Ancient Celtic priest
18 Gambler's st.
19 Letter encls.
20 Grocery clerk's privileges?
23 Get on
24 551, to Augustus
25 Meet, as an occasion
28 Big name in baby food
30 Gloater's cry
32 ___ double take
33 Long-winded saga on audio-cassette?
36 Baja blue
39 Kind of ear or hat
40 Tolkien creatures
41 Certain fish fin bones?
46 Article in *Le Devoir*
47 NBA MVP Steve
48 Stands for sittings
52 More than fear
54 Cloddish fool
55 Mauna ___
56 Cry from a desolate lane?
60 April 1st antic
62 News letters?
63 Bay window
64 ___ deux (ballet duet)
65 ___ Tin Tin
66 Tush
67 Glass fragment: Var.
68 Nobody special
69 Puts food on the table

DOWN

1 Elderly woman, derogatorily
2 Rummage for food
3 Over-charging merchant
4 "I don't give ___"
5 "Good thinking. Not!"
6 Mushrooms and mould
7 0 letters
8 Sitarist Shankar
9 Redeeming, with "in"
10 ___ Can (fed. dept.)
11 Turned down
12 Mined matter
13 McCourt memoir
21 US worker's agcy.
22 Sheepish look
26 Toy train signal
27 Stately trees
29 OPEC units
30 Tchaikovsky's middle name
31 Jester's gesture
34 Furnace output: Abbr.
35 Porgy's partner
36 Come up against
37 *Titanic* villain Billy
38 Computer consumers, collectively
42 Rapped
43 Bobbies' fink
44 ___-majesté
45 Oven-scrubber's aid
49 Paige of the stage
50 Like most econo-models
51 Struthers and Field
53 Time off, briefly
54 Madame Chrétien
57 Big do
58 Eagles' "___ Eyes"
59 Hebridean hillside
60 Letter ender: Abbr.
61 Encouraging word

33 *I's in Here*

ACROSS

1 Oodles
5 *The ___ of Night* (early soap)
9 Wipe out
14 *Little Women* little woman
15 Nada, once
16 Good packers
17 Landscapist Emily
18 Mad melee
20 Ravi Shankar's double-barrelled instrument?
22 Moon state
23 Parallel ending?
24 Northeast Indian state
27 Not done as well
29 Part of CPA: Abbr.
32 Be a good host, say
34 My, in Matane
35 "___ one am not . . ."
36 Comparison used by da Vinci's model?
39 Not even ___ of hope
40 Gold measures: Abbr.
41 Bon vivant's gift
42 Dutch van follower
43 Tie between dog and owner

45 Graff of *Mr. Belvedere*
46 US feminist Lucretia
47 Ratio words
49 Out-of-towner's rant?
54 "See?"
56 "Don't blame ___ me"
57 Need for a word?
58 Dodge car
59 Terrarium dweller
60 Girly boy
61 Word sung with champagne
62 French people

DOWN

1 Mr. Dressup teachings
2 Actress Pinsent
3 Manuel's other
4 Don't recycle
5 Finally: Fr.
6 Big needle user
7 Peck, to pals
8 Stye and sty?
9 Stratford thespian, maybe
10 Like farmland
11 Banned apple spray
12 It's on "la table"
13 New Canadian's course: Abbr.

19 Lout's lack
21 Sri Lankan
24 Equally irked
25 Shell site
26 Sub's guide
28 Congregate
29 In need of water, perhaps
30 Blues/rocker James
31 Early Greek hub
33 "Good effort"
35 On bended knee
37 CBC Radio One and Two, e.g.
38 "Lord, ___?" (Last Supper question)
43 Musician's forte
44 Flirts with
46 Spies who spy on spies
48 Wall or wash starter
49 Hauls behind
50 Chop ___
51 To ___ (just so)
52 Blue, but not green
53 Sinusitis specialists: Abbr.
54 Hosp. hook-ups
55 A ___ (yours): Fr.

■ DAVE MACLEOD

34 *Let It B*E**

ACROSS
1 BRITISH COLUMBIA RAPTOR
10 Taken ___ (surprised)
15 Grizzly kin
16 Call word
17 Pink slip pay
18 ___ *ed Euridice* (Gluck opera)
19 "Telephone Line" band
20 List ender
22 Scam decoys
25 Capri ending
26 Strange prefix
28 Scottish pattern
30 Smoothed, as a dirt road
32 *Exodus* hero
33 Awestruck sound
36 Love, Italian-style
37 MELEE REMINDERS
40 Pewter, for one
43 Unit of contraband
44 Tire layer
47 Cajoled
49 Shade source
52 Chant ending
53 Ewe's mate
56 Ballerina Kain and skater Magnussen
57 Actress Bankhead
60 Put down, in slang
61 Margaret ___ Thatcher
62 Keeping apart
66 Dot in the ocean
67 Marshall McLuhan's interest
68 Dear in Dorval
69 UNPLEASANT CONCLUSION

DOWN
1 Air rifle ammo
2 You ___ Here
3 2002 PGA champion Davis
4 Inhabits
5 Sign up
6 "The ___ Daba Honeymoon"
7 Item in a pool
8 Milk, in combinations
9 Having good posture
10 On ___ streak (winning)
11 LAWYER'S HURDLES
12 Made with a cream sauce
13 More to Felix Unger's liking
14 Kitchy- ___
21 Head lines?
22 Masseuse's workplace
23 When doubled, a derisive laugh
24 Nintendo rival
27 Shelley creation
29 Gab
31 Sally Field role Norma ___
34 Visit Mont Tremblant
35 Soccer great
37 TYPE OF MAPLE
38 Soapmaking need
39 Hollandaise sauce ingredient
40 Royal flush card
41 Ill-mannered
42 French explorer of Canada
44 Take the chair
45 Guitarist Breau, for short
46 What a nod means
48 Joanne of *Abie's Irish Rose*
50 Bovary, for one
51 More time-worn
54 Out on ___
55 Kenyan tribesman
58 Past due
59 Emcee
61 Sot's sound
63 D-Day transport
64 *Under a Glass Bell* author
65 Gallivant

35 *Odd Couples*

ACROSS

1 Baker's dozen?
5 Mikhail's wife
10 Hose woe
14 A word from Mork
15 Pavlova and Karina
16 ___ way, shape or form
17 "When I was ___ I served . . . ("HMS Pinafore")
18 Area measure
19 Forbidden fruit locale
20 Native warrior with a faint heart?
23 Place for a polar bear
24 Veer off course
25 Fabric pile
28 Waiter's place, often: Abbr.
29 ___ Crunch
32 Nursery item
34 Starring roles for *Anne of Green Gables* actress Megan?
36 "___ long way to Tipperary . . ."
39 Word of wonder
40 Dab at, as a stain
41 Surgery assistant with a calm demeanour?

46 Military hub of Ancient Greece
47 "Touché" sayer's weapon
48 Carte start
51 Not 'neath
52 See ___ glance
54 Childish chatter
56 It'll be wrapped up by next Christmas?
60 Petticoat
62 Calgary Stampede event
63 Murray of song
64 La vie lead-in
65 Female friends in Québec
66 Hockey's Larionov
67 Dwarves' refrain
68 Potato pancake
69 Prides' places

DOWN

1 Puts into law
2 Oafish brute
3 Work at, as a bone
4 Darfur's country
5 Short end of the stick
6 Indigo-yielding plant
7 ___ 500
8 Didn't act
9 Gurus' getaways
10 Capital of Ukraine
11 Saying it isn't so

12 SSW's reverse
13 ___-*Tiki*
21 Rich to Ricardo
22 Off-base, in a way
26 Montreal rocker ___ Nova
27 Bug in one's ear, say
30 Scheme
31 Not a soul
33 Brigitte's baby
34 Not quite middling
35 Beat but good
36 Facto intro
37 Drywaller's need
38 SpongeBob's pal Patrick, for one
42 State in French?
43 Redford's baseball movie, with *The*
44 "Only in Canada" brew
45 Desert-dry
48 Get even for
49 "Imagine" songwriter
50 Takes in, maybe
53 Bakery draw
55 Reiterator's words
57 "I've had it ___ here"
58 Take out, maybe
59 Pre-Christmas no-no
60 Learning inst.
61 Maui memento

36 *K2 Expedition*

ACROSS

1 It's just over a foot
6 Bro
9 Chapters in history
13 ___ Work ('80s band)
14 I, to Claudius
15 Stale Italian bread?
16 Winter coat
18 In a refined manner
20 Chokers
22 Arias, for example
23 Shows curiosity
24 Hooey
25 Flesh and blood
26 Winter melons
28 Inc. up here
31 Camera name at the K2 summit
34 Not a lot, but . . .
36 Corrida combatants
38 Slangy hot dogs
39 Loss of this makes an ion
41 Place to get K2 expedition news
42 Long March leader
43 Loss of this means extinction
45 Pushrod pusher
46 ___ Perce (Northwest Native)
47 Actor Tamiroff
51 Convention handout
54 Bases for busts
56 *Fathers and Sons* novelist
58 Stuck it out
59 *Peter Pan* pirate
60 Chowed down
61 Heavenly prefix
62 Copycat
63 Scrooge outburst
64 Levees

DOWN

1 Name on a fridge
2 Hawaiian geese
3 Sound at the K2 base camp door
4 Escapades
5 Bibliography: Abbr.
6 Old dinero
7 Many moons
8 El Al destination
9 Sir John of rock
10 Metis revolutionary
11 Patron of Alice
12 What Simon does
17 K2 mountain-range name, appropriately
19 Opinionated start
21 Lettuce variety
25 K2 summit assaulters, it may seem
26 Punic Wars side
27 Part of a kowtow, often
28 Clark's crush
29 Arduous journey
30 Place ___ Arts, Montréal
31 Caffeine-laden nut
32 Black-and-white bite
33 Santa's mo.
35 6 on a handset
36 Pro ___
37 Blubber
40 Assyrian capital
44 Mack of *The Original Amateur Hour*
45 Any Raptor
47 Arcade game name
48 Why bring this? K2's rivers are made of ice!
49 *Prince Valiant* princess
50 Windows forerunner
51 Start of a new parent's shout
52 Eyesore, usually
53 Natural air conditioner
54 Fur haters, briefly
55 Macho man
57 Slap the cuffs on

■ DAVE MACLEOD

37 *The Joke's on You*

ACROSS
1 Your reps in Ottawa
4 Golfing goals
8 Urges forward
14 Heavy-metal rock
15 Trapped like ___
16 "Gangsta's Paradise" rapper
17 Covers breaking news
19 Words of resignation
20 Three Stooges' props
22 Wall St. letters
23 Tactics
24 He plays Grissom on *CSI*
29 A pittance, slangily
32 *Top Hat* star
34 Had on
35 Red Skelton lapel prop
39 1950s TV private eye Peter
40 ___ *Claiborne* (Stephen King bestseller)
41 You might pick it up, if you're generous
42 Tilted
45 Lovett and Waggoner
47 Cod kin
51 Burlesque props
57 Get the job done
58 Qualifies
59 Ethylene is one
60 Quit, as a motor
61 Big shoebox letters
62 Salad preparer, maybe
63 Where el sol rises
64 *Treasure Island* initials

DOWN
1 ___ David kosher wine
2 Shareholder's substitute
3 Trickles
4 ___ Alto, CA
5 Parched
6 Sitarist Shankar
7 WWII British submachine gun
8 Eaves dropper?
9 It's usually slow in TV replays
10 Bess's partner in a Gershwin musical
11 Sewing machine inventor
12 He's prone to being prone
13 Repairs the outfield
18 Missed the alarm
21 Family docs
25 Corn serving
26 ___ for tat
27 "___ Tu" (Verdi aria)
28 Tears apart
30 Greek war god
31 "So's ___ old man!"
32 Water colour
33 Lotion ingredients, often
34 Meriting the price
35 Certain NCO
36 "Well ___ darn it!"
37 State with keys: Abbr.
38 Horror actor Chaney
42 Like much of Glacier National Park
43 Wobble
44 Enzyme's end
46 They keep the teams in line
48 Many an Internet user
49 Use a prie-dieu
50 Mountain roads, in places
51 "Come again?"
52 Head band?
53 Surrender, as territory
54 Les États- ___
55 Proofreader's notation
56 Keep out of sight

38 Old MacDonald's Farm

ACROSS

1 McCourt title ___ *Ashes*
8 Gain entry to
14 Seriously determined
15 Shrugger's comment
16 Where one might see a tailgater
18 "Yippee!!"
19 Mas' mates
20 Poop out
21 "Get ___!" ("Smarten up!")
24 Québec town Val-___
25 Expectant dad, maybe
26 Heckling session on the Hill, at times
29 Salt Lake City state
30 It starts le 21 juin
31 Online chuckle
32 Certain serpent
33 You-here link, on a map
34 "Well, let me think . . ."
35 ___ Mahal
38 Hire a prosecuter
39 ___ Paulo, Brazil
40 Hawaiian port with an oxymoronic name
41 Lacking depth, as a character
45 Mac tack-on
46 Hosp. hookups
47 A-bomb experiment
48 Lack of effort
49 Stand buy
50 Communication for the deaf: Abbr.
51 "Enter" or "exit," on a script
56 "Hubba hubba!"
57 Agreement between countries
58 Introductory: Abbr.
59 Holding the most water

DOWN

1 ___ Lingus (Ireland's carrier)
2 Scot's not
3 Like salt-and-pepper hair: Var.
4 Captivated
5 Import tax
6 "Do ___ say!"
7 Beginner's beginning
8 Has in one's sights
9 Roman 401
10 Curb, as bad behaviour
11 Singer Iglesias (son of Julio)
12 Was elbowed in bed, maybe
13 More bitter
17 Record problem
21 Water colour
22 Raw courage
23 Cut the crop
24 Pamper, with "on"
25 It's a ball
27 Able was ___ saw Elba
28 "Tickle-me" dolls
33 Autobahn auto
34 Famed fairy-tale writer's first name
35 Pea picker-upper
36 Word said with a sigh
37 Effect of espresso
38 Dakar's country, in SW Africa
39 Lopped
40 Distressed caller's connection
41 Figure of speech?
42 "___ is final until you are satisfied"
43 Noon, in Québec
44 Orthopedist's sole concern
45 "The Tortoise and the Hare" writer
49 Early man
50 Entr'___ (intermission)
52 Inventor Whitney
53 Benz ending
54 Tie breakers: Abbr.
55 Bottom line

39 *It's About Time*

ACROSS

1 Go on a diet
5 Albertville abode
11 Library reminder, perhaps
14 Saintly luminescence
15 ___ *Hot Tin Roof*
16 Besides
17 Scientist's timekeeper
19 Have the deed to
20 Jimjams
21 End of peace?
22 Eton student
24 Bigfoot relatives
26 Fluctuated
27 Go along (with)
30 Singer's syllable
31 Start of a 2/14 request
34 Poetic nightfall
35 Went bad
38 Greek war god
39 ___ the hills (ancient)
41 Totally gross
42 Wicker, essentially
44 Believer's suffix
45 Cows and sows
46 Kind of dance tune
47 Hawaiian VIP
49 Paradigm of deadness

52 Put on the books
56 Groups of nine
57 Fallen space station
59 Rob Roy's rejection
60 Sign of summer
61 Latin for "Time flies!"
64 Skye cap
65 Votes in
66 Day saver
67 Consumed
68 Begins
69 Flin ___, Manitoba

DOWN

1 Disreputable
2 Coffee house order
3 Player's lament
4 Tattoo word
5 301 in Old Rome
6 Curler's pushoff point
7 Iceland's ocean: Abbr.
8 Hemlock ___ (forest pest)
9 *Le Devoir* ink
10 Begins liking
11 Coach's timekeeper
12 Meeker of hockey
13 Sharpened
18 Words before many words

23 Taking sides
25 Withering look
26 Ancient's timekeeper
28 Light gas
29 Cartoon collectible
31 Lush surroundings
32 Cenozoic or Paleozoic
33 Musician's timekeeper
35 VW precursors
36 Scratch (out)
37 Functional start?
40 Racquet wood
43 Dad's brothers, for instance
47 Destiny
48 Spongy stuff
49 Much of Vancouver, topographically
50 ___ a time (singly)
51 Fred Astaire's sister
53 Child who behaves perfectly
54 City near Giza
55 Range of the Rockies
57 Pound pick, probably
58 Playground retort
62 Mac alternatives
63 TV channels 14 and up

40 *Pipe Down!*

ACROSS

1 Speaks one's views
7 Whale group
10 When doubled, a vodka drink
13 Winter Olympics city, 1998
14 A handful
15 VCR button
16 ". . . ___ sleeping, Brother John . . ."
17 Place for a pitchfork
19 Puts in planters
20 Title word in a 1994 Morgan Freeman film
22 He made many great hits
23 Prefix meaning "nerve"
24 Capital on a fjord
26 Back in
28 Egg-on-sidewalk sound
31 Needs to go to the pix?
32 Sherpa's journeys
34 Emphatic refusal
36 Wool gathering?
39 Salon froth
40 Beginning
41 Lions' club: Abbr.
42 "___ coffee?"
44 Mark the start of, with "in"
48 Mikita of hockey
50 Have a hunch?
52 Worldwide workers' assn.
53 Large section in Imelda Marcos' closet?
56 Trump game with 32 cards
57 Items on a 53-Across
58 Feign a cold by coughing, say
60 A language of Thailand
61 Trees for which many streets are named
62 Fore'er and e'er
63 Ant.
64 ___ Dawn Chong
65 Divining rod

DOWN

1 Equal in ability
2 Jailbird's early out
3 Utterance when the light goes on
4 Some votes on the Hill
5 Antacid brand
6 Andy Capp, for one
7 Risk being court-martialled
8 Gospel's Grant, and others
9 Hockey netting
10 Toller on skates
11 Harassing a performer
12 "Gross!"
14 Skilled marksmen
18 Confucian path
21 Ear coverings
23 Plight of the wicked
25 Gravy maker's cube
27 They may be rural at Can. Post
29 Santa ___ (hot winds)
30 Annulled a contract, maybe
33 Sporting sword
35 Louse larvae
36 Liquid hand cleanser
37 Hip-py craze?
38 Sign up in the States
39 Roast hosts
43 "What ___" ("Too bad")
45 They often have an uphill climb
46 *Seinfeld* gal
47 Wicked one
49 "I'm being sarcastic!"
51 Rubbed out
54 Pitcher in a painting
55 Actress Ward
56 Put a slant on
57 Andy Capp's wife
59 From ___ Z (the gamut)

■ DAVE MACLEOD

41 *Airborne Animals*

ACROSS

1 Large ale cask
4 Played a high, arcing tennis shot
10 October birthstone
14 Sudbury paydirt
15 Bullfight cheer
16 Hole in the skin
17 Winter hrs. in Prince George
18 Chess World Champion Anatoly
19 ___ *la Douce*
20 Common arachnids that don't use webs
23 Stick in the fridge
24 Whitney or Wallach
25 Dictator Amin
27 Motel alternative
29 High times
31 *Star Wars* baddie Darth
33 Old Dodge
35 Burning Spear's music
36 Bullwinkle's friend Rocky, et al.
41 Pee Wee and Della
42 Strike callers
43 Guy with his back to the world
44 Beaufort, for one
45 Tickle pink
50 Designer monogram
51 Game similar to Crazy Eights
53 "Out ___?" (poker query)
54 Little Orphan Annie's outburst
60 Skirt that goes below the knee
61 It's just one thing after another
62 Sapporo sash
63 Cheese that's made backwards?
64 Makes up (for)
65 Barrister's accessory
66 Comes down with
67 "A-Tisket, A- ___ "
68 Greyhound stop: Abbr.

DOWN

1 Prime Minister is one
2 First "Bond girl" Andress
3 Male tennis stars
4 Mischievous Norse god
5 *The Good Earth* heroine
6 *Titanic* sinker
7 Dances to jazz
8 Chooses the window instead of the aisle
9 He's in the details
10 Mayberry boy
11 Oatmeal
12 Government sale, sometimes
13 Idyllic spot
21 Whale group
22 Multi-faceted
26 Makes angry
28 Studies hard
29 Young '___ (kids)
30 Excite, as curiosity
32 Farmer's field?: Abbr.
34 Sporty British autos
35 Saw with the grain
36 Skirmish
37 Decide it doesn't matter
38 Chewed out
39 "This ___ test"
40 Thurman of *Dangerous Liaisons*
44 Mozart piece
46 Mauna ___ (Hawaiian volcano)
47 One-way indicators
48 Piece of tabloid gossip
49 Naval banner
52 Try to bite, puppy-style
55 Intents
56 Large in La Salle
57 Very thin
58 French conception
59 Gusto
60 Canadian actress Tilly

42 *Inflation Pressure*

ACROSS

1 Fabergé collectible
4 Mine, to Mimi
8 Praised to the skies
14 Proceeding in a tedious fashion
16 Make hopping mad
17 When it's inflated, it floats on air
19 Olympic swords
20 Metric verse
21 Big Apple ballpark
22 "Yes ___, Bob!"
23 British seat
27 When it's inflated, profit is more likely
30 Short suckers
31 Absolutely no way
32 Buddy who's a communist
36 They fired Dan Rather
38 Like queens and drones
39 At the drop of ___
40 When it's inflated, you're the best
45 Baby bouncer
46 Keep an ___ the ground
47 Knock down
50 Chance to hit
51 Pago Pago locale
52 When it's inflated, our interest rates go up
57 Some things are best left in it
58 Grab in a hurry
59 Like the Dead Sea
60 Medieval Italian fortress site
61 Its in Iberville

DOWN

1 Book after Galatians in the New Testament: Abbr.
2 It's written in stone
3 Run for a Hail Mary pass
4 Big commotions
5 Russian fighter
6 Modest beachwear
7 Shrugs off
8 Cups and saucers, maybe
9 Nothing more than
10 Web address, for short
11 Eastern "way"
12 Type of trip
13 Cubs' home
15 Bleak, in verse
18 They're 38-Across
22 Tropical fish
23 End of grace
24 All-night party
25 Bouillabaisse, e.g.
26 Auction enders
28 A former Mrs. Trump
29 Most tech schools, e.g.
32 Big wine tun
33 Golf tournament for pros and amateurs
34 Eminem's "8 ___"
35 BC political commentator Mair
36 Personal properties
37 Scott of *Charles in Charge*
39 Sort
41 Tiny in Trois-Rivières
42 Sunscreen stuff
43 Hersey's bell town
44 New things that don't work, slangily
48 Title for Dumas's Edmond Dantès
49 Knocks down for good
50 Chief Yemeni port
51 Not all
52 IV amts.
53 King or carte start
54 Cambodia's Lon ___
55 Do-do link
56 Army bed

43 *Play It Again*

ACROSS

1 Largest city in China
9 Offerer of green eggs and ham
15 DON'T TAKE PRECAUTIONS
16 Canadian singer Marshall ("Let it Rain")
17 Rater's scale, often
18 Get back
19 Baseball's Slaughter
21 Frazier's brother
22 THIS IS ONE
26 It makes a short vowel long
28 Sun's rays, in short
29 Brief blurb
30 Employ
31 Masochistic beginning
35 SECRET SPY MISSION
39 Work without ___
40 Time sheet: Abbr.
41 Pago Pago locale
42 "Come on, ___ sport"
43 Canadiens' conference
45 PHRASE ABOUT A CERTAIN SHELL VENDOR, FOR ONE
50 Cost ___ and a leg
51 Some sushi fare
52 In a pleasant way
54 High divers' areas
60 Pigged out
61 COMMENT TO A COUCH POTATO, MAYBE
62 Walk ___ (tread very carefully)
63 Surround oneself (in)

DOWN

1 Sign of a sellout
2 Attila, notably
3 Prop suffix
4 King Cole of song
5 Miracle-___ (garden brand)
6 Carling O'Keefe's Extra Old Stock, familiarly
7 In ___ (somewhat)
8 Empathetic remark
9 Mediterranean isl.
10 Modifies
11 A witch's is black
12 Totalled up
13 Farewell, to François
14 Minister's estate
20 Bar fixture
22 Garlic unit
23 Convened again
24 ___ about (roughly)
25 Camp sight?
26 Stray's haven
27 Dumbbell at the gym
30 Good points
31 Washington, but not Lincoln
32 To love, in Toulouse
33 It's ___ die
34 ___ even keel
36 You of yore
37 Speechify
38 Right-hand man: Abbr.
42 Lame excuse?
43 Shania's real name
44 Good points
45 *Last ___ in Paris*
46 Something to cry over
47 Mother-of-pearl
48 Canadian pollster Allan
49 Golfer's pitching iron
53 CFL stats
55 ___-Man (video game)
56 Jeff Lynne's group, initially
57 Henry Miller lover
58 RAF honour
59 "Savvy?"

■ DAVE MACLEOD

44 *How's Your Old Man?*

ACROSS

1 Those annoying you, to you
7 Name on a power tool
11 Cape Town's ctry.
14 Long for
15 Is next in line
17 Like a clock with hands
18 Brought pressure to bear
19 "Git!"
21 Good, in slang
24 Church bench
25 Idyllic setting
26 Thrown for ___
28 Switch positions
31 "Give it ___!"
33 Rice-a-___
34 Hooey
36 Theatre treat
41 Knitted things
42 Cap-___ (head-to-foot)
43 Neutral hues
46 Bit of granola
47 Technical data
48 Ireland's ___ Lingus
49 Caribou kin
51 Circus sight
52 Batman and Robin, now that they're retired?
59 Discreet exit site
60 Big rig fuel
64 Thoroughbred's strong point
65 Like wicked ski runs
66 "You called?"
67 Jeanne et Thérèse: Abbr.
68 College application parts

DOWN

1 *High Sierra* star Lupino
2 Place to kick back
3 "This ___ test"
4 Slick
5 Marches in formation
6 Smooth transition in radio
7 Old suture material
8 Support for a proposal
9 "___ no idea!"
10 Olin of *Havana*
11 Brain stumper
12 Wraps for ladies
13 Comparable to a pin?
16 Like BC cedar
20 Took an oath about
21 Pointed remark
22 Ex-Expo Moises
23 "Stop that!"
27 Wait patiently
29 Gymnast Comaneci
30 Heaven's gatekeeper
31 Saint Moritz sight
32 Make a long story short
34 Like a Canadien or a Canuck
35 How-___ (learner's tips)
37 Greek goddess of the dawn
38 Dentist's order
39 Post-wedding fling?
40 Place to pick up chicks
43 *The Great* ___ (F. Scott Fitzgerald)
44 Do an electrical upgrade
45 Wears away
47 Supplies for 41-Across
50 Mountain hideaway
53 Fixed charge
54 Contributes
55 "Nothing ___!"
56 Perfect
57 Units of energy
58 Red and Black
61 Mexicali Mrs.
62 TV Tarzan Ron
63 Fleur-de-___

45 *Prefix-ation*

ACROSS

1 CBC's *The ___ Estate*
6 Eighth Commandment no-no
11 Alphabet run
14 Integra maker
15 Creditor's contacts
16 Boy from Bristol
17 18-wheeler with new radials?
19 Come to a conclusion
20 ___ *and Crake* (Atwood)
21 Out
22 Dawdling
23 Tel Aviv's ctry.
25 Writer ___ Boothe Luce
27 Was introduced to Madame Curie?
32 Uplifting lingerie item
34 Pop of punk
35 ___ plume
36 Admires greatly
38 Librarian's book woe
40 Shake like ___
41 Has a bawl
42 Alias intro
43 Language usage of a Nicaraguan guerilla?
47 Lew who played Dr. Kildare

48 Start to cycle
49 Sporran go-with
52 Brainstorms
54 Flat screen monitors, for short
58 Here, in Hull
59 Built-in cutting board, say?
61 Brewer's vat
62 Horseracing site or a tie worn there
63 ___ one's mind (calmed)
64 Atlantic shopper's addnl. cost
65 Movers and shakers
66 Works like a beaver

DOWN

1 Mi-la bridge
2 Cake finisher
3 Emitting noxious gas
4 *Hi and Lois* baby
5 Sound of laughter
6 "... and ___ bed" (Pepys)
7 Like a dreaming dog, maybe
8 In a spooky way
9 Where Leafs gather
10 '60s drug
11 Asp's target

12 Dark and damp
13 Whirling water
18 Get one's goat
22 Rio Grande feeder
24 Chinese menu choice
26 Welcomes, as a new year
27 Hotshot
28 Some movie ratings
29 "In other words . . ."
30 Mt. Rushmore's state
31 Trillion: Prefix
32 Bric-à-___
33 Move, in realtor-speak
37 Plague with worry
38 Bespectacled dwarf
39 Like a wide angle
41 Submissive Spanish reply
44 Musical piece meaning airy
45 Come to a conclusion
46 Engine tray
49 Kin kin
50 Places for MDs and RNs
51 It's caught in a trap
53 Some solicitors, for short
55 Castro's home
56 Nancy of teen mystery
57 Norms: Abbr.
59 Creep
60 Gas pump: Abbr.

■ DAVE MACLEOD

46 *Headake*

ACROSS

1 Switch positions
4 A good one has a lot of tips
10 Ontario is one
14 Barrister's field
15 Truth ___ (kids' game)
16 Ocean birds of Greenland
17 Way to go
18 Larionov's land
19 Small fraction of a min.
20 Result of faulty reasoning
23 Kofi ___ Annan
24 Positive votes: Var.
25 Emails
27 The ones here
29 Piano keys, slangily
31 Tsunami cause, usually
35 Ticked off
36 Ray of light
38 ___ plea (bargain)
42 Comment at a Uri Geller show
47 Near
49 Entry papers
50 Number after sei
51 Sign of a sellout
54 Back muscles, for short
55 "Twist and Shout" lyric

59 "Do ___ else!"
60 Stop daydreaming
61 Uneven?
63 Harness race pace
64 Catching Z's
65 Trent Reznor's band: Abbr.
66 Being on it is corrupt, with "the"
67 Spirited rides
68 Psychologist/columnist LeShan

DOWN

1 Pay add-on
2 Camp fuel
3 One in a sauna
4 *Star Trek* Klingon
5 Resort island off Venezuela
6 "You can bet on that!"
7 Chores
8 Fort ___, Ontario
9 Deciphered
10 Banks, at times
11 Old talk-show host Hall
12 Dough preparer
13 PC panic button
21 Not fizzle out

22 Bar opener?
23 Absorbed, as losses
26 Heading from North Bay to Toronto: Abbr.
28 Canadian speech mannerisms
29 Trendy furniture store
30 Wiener schnitzel meat
32 Pack it in
33 Golden Rule word
34 Tummy muscles
37 1055 in Old Rome
38 IV units
39 Dietary fat substitute
40 Old kitchen hanger
41 Phoenician love goddess
43 Sportswear brand
44 Dry comparison
45 Kind of grasshopper
46 Chicane shape
48 Comic-book scream
51 Shopworn
52 Kathmandu currency
53 Chose, with "for"
56 Those, to José
57 Technical sch.
58 Conks on the head
59 Addams Family cousin
62 Paternity determiner

47 *Pun Intended*

ACROSS
1 Tease
4 Nintendo needs
7 Fauna members
14 True to form
16 "Forget it!"
17 Start of a punny quip
19 Shiny cotton fabric
20 ___ precedent (is the first of its kind)
21 %: Abbr.
23 Fort sites
26 Worked (up)
27 Some Greek letters
30 Crackpot
33 CFB rank
34 One who loves a lot
36 Middle of the quip
40 Call from the threshold
41 Windows forerunner
43 Advertiser
46 Chair men?
47 Shade at the beach?
48 When Macbeth sees visions of his future
51 Type of lettuce
52 Nevertheless, for short
55 Sign up
58 End of the quip
63 Bitches and vixens
64 It may be pencilled or plucked
65 Good place to start
66 Esteemed mil. honour
67 Ron who played TV's Tarzan

DOWN
1 Squeal on, with "out"
2 "It ___" (reply to "Who's there?")
3 Bad advice
4 Hairdresser's handful
5 They drive fancy cars
6 More crafty: Var.
7 Solution: Abbr.
8 Cambodia's Lon ___
9 Wife of Osiris
10 Lester Pearson's nickname
11 R & B's Franklin
12 Property rentals
13 So-called Chamber of Sober Second Thought
15 Mariner's milieu
18 Regina-to-Prince Albert dir.
21 Tammy Faye's grp.
22 "Pet" plant
24 Internet message
25 Catch a wave
28 2006 Winter Olympics city
29 Matter make-up
31 ___ *of Endearment*
32 Puppy love
34 Multiple-choice choices
35 Ba-___! (punchline emphasis)
37 Command to Nellie
38 "My word!"
39 Mower maker
42 Sound made by a defensive cat
43 Flagpoles, e.g.
44 Warehouse platform
45 Neither early nor late
46 Sunbeams
49 Toothbrush brand
50 "When ___ You" (Leo Sayer)
53 Mound
54 1952 Winter Olympics city
56 Fuel-trading grp.
57 Neighbour of Syr.
59 Singer/songwriter Cohen, to friends
60 Expert finish?
61 Mustard or Klink: Abbr.
62 Trans-Canada, for one: Abbr.

48 Governor General's Literary Award

ACROSS

1 Welles role (1941)
5 Doris Day lyric
9 One of a Disney duo
14 Bug-eyed
15 ___ all-time low
16 Winding river feature
17 Latin wheel
18 Emphasize, in a way
20 Receiver of the puzzle title (1971)
22 Seasonal song opener
23 Stumblebum
24 To be in Chibougamau
25 *The Simpsons* storekeeper
27 Web help list, for short
29 OK Corral combatant
33 From the top
36 Litigious challenge
40 Giver of the puzzle title (1967–74)
43 Fastened, as a winter coat
44 Conductor Klemperer
45 Lévesque of Québec
46 Came upon
48 Rugby score
50 Rib donor
53 Something lent or bent
56 As required, after "if"
61 Receiver of the puzzle title (1972)
64 Eric Clapton highlight
65 Tolkien giants
66 Two foursomes
67 Online publication
68 Hourly fee
69 Peanuts, essentially
70 Grounded jets
71 *Jurassic Park* menace, familiarly

DOWN

1 Destiny
2 ". . . and that's ___ thing." (Martha Stewart)
3 Word in Québec town names
4 Quaint oath
5 Place for bouillabaisse
6 Sicilian smoker
7 Michael Enright's medium
8 End of ___
9 Pear type
10 Public revenues overseer
11 Like ___ from the blue
12 More achy
13 "___ best he speak no harm of Brutus here." (Julius Caesar)
19 Feature of 64-Across
21 Trudeau listing: Abbr.
26 Handy word processor command
28 Baseball bat wood
29 ___ "Kookie" Byrnes of *77 Sunset Strip*
30 Jackie's second
31 Netman Laver
32 Took a nosedive
34 CPR giver
35 Gold-medal skater Katarina
37 Dir. from Sydney to Glace Bay, Cape Breton
38 Brando's film debut, with *The*
39 Before, before
41 Friend of Tarzan
42 Boardwalk snacks
47 Prefix meaning "four"
49 Affirmative vote
50 Toronto gridders
51 *Irma la ___*
52 Have ___ of (taste)
54 Pack carriers
55 Count for a realtor
57 Chris of the court
58 Iranian bread
59 Ms. Midler
60 Big-selling 1920s car
62 Charlie Brown's expletive
63 The Arctic Circle and environs: Abbr.

■ BARBARA OLSON

49 *Seeing Things*

ACROSS

1 US worker's ID
4 Make a new impression
10 Pre-high sch.
14 Lucy of *Charlie's Angels*
15 Part of a plaint by Juliet
16 Canadian dictionary
17 Shock treatment: Abbr.
18 "Ready?"
19 Pontiac muscle cars
20 Have one's 69-Across on
23 Marshmallow melt
24 Verbal thumbs-ups
25 Mac tack-on
29 Secure a shoelace
32 Key out
35 Keep one's 69-Across out
38 Croat or Serb
40 Mario's brother, at the arcade
41 Scientologist Hubbard
42 Keep one's 69-Across on
44 Pan Am rival, once
45 Ohm symbol
46 Guadalajaran girls: Abbr.
49 "Would you care to?" lazily
52 Sunni and Shia, e.g.
56 Run one's 69-Across over
61 Light lunch locale

62 ___ motel (rendezvous site)
63 ___-Magnon
64 Questions
65 Ancient Mesopotamian city
66 P.O. box item
67 Servile reply
68 Last six lines of a sonnet
69 See 20, 35, 42 and 56-Across

DOWN

1 Yukon transportation
2 Command to Cujo
3 Severely crazed
4 Bengali bigmouth, for one
5 Mystery's Stanley Gardner
6 Slim cigar brand
7 Playground retort
8 Having poor drainage
9 From head ___
10 Kind of white
11 Racer's disadvantage
12 Inflatable headgear?
13 Goof (up)
21 Writer Levin
22 Delhi wrap
26 Di or da preceder

27 Prefix meaning "nerve"
28 They creep around old buildings
30 "___ pronounce you . . ."
31 Sicilian smoker
32 This, in Tijuana
33 Close huffily
34 Easy endeavours
36 Ghoulish aide
37 Special knack
39 Practice of eating no animal products
43 Unwanted flight info: Abbr.
47 Comparable to a pancake
48 Common "épice"
50 Hawaiian state birds
51 Dwelling
53 Participate in a triathlon
54 Liable to make one pucker
55 Keep for later
56 Down under "howdy"
57 ___-majesty (high treason)
58 Paperboy's concerns
59 Superlative ending
60 "What ___ is new?"

50 *Give'Em a Hand*

ACROSS

1 DJ's assortment
4 Light ___
9 Make sense
14 Little chuckle
15 17th-century English philosopher John
16 They're prudish
17 Santa ___ winds
18 Went out with
19 Forms a puddle
20 Picks someone from the lineup
23 Breakaway country from Ethiopia (1993)
24 One or more
25 In order (to)
26 Easy marks
28 Army eatery
32 Nile goddess
34 Latin list ender
36 Whip-cracking movement
41 Astronomical distance
42 Hindu princess
43 Petty quarrel
44 ___ *Arabian Nights*
46 The CIBC will send you one: Abbr.
50 ___ Salvador
51 Controls of a sort
54 It leaves a bad taste in one's mouth
59 School course that's a snap
60 Prickly plants
61 Biol. or chem.
62 Bothered
63 ". . . the broad side of ___ "
64 Place to stand a round
65 Alan Ladd oater classic (1953)
66 Hicks
67 Superlative ending

DOWN

1 Rubs the wrong way
2 *Meet the Parents* star
3 Canada's Twain
4 Birch relative
5 ". . . sweet, and ___ you"
6 Behaves like
7 Home furnishings chain
8 CN station employee, once
9 Put to use
10 Plummet
11 Designer Christian
12 Unattractive fruit (and sounds like it)
13 "Hey, over here!"
21 Sporty car styles
22 Invisible
27 Elroy Jetson's dog
28 Fold, spindle or mutilate
29 Lilly of pharmaceuticals
30 Family girl
31 Took a chair
32 Tina Turner's ex
33 Get-together at church
35 Lead-in for light or night
36 Speed of sound unit: Abbr.
37 You stand to lose this?
38 Cohen biographer Nadel
39 Winnipeg winter hrs.
40 Cry "Taxi!"
45 Like a small garage
46 U-turn from NNE
47 "Can ___?" (incredulous query)
48 Centres of devotion
49 Casual cover-up
50 Perform like Elvis
52 ___ nous (between us)
53 Tennis scores after deuce
54 Tavern inventory
55 Sodium hydroxide, in the lab
56 Davis Cup grp.
57 Printer's blue
58 He debuted in *Elephant Boy* (1937)

51 *Somewhere a Dog Braked*

ACROSS

1 Clumsy clod
4 ___ *Miller* (Verdi opera)
9 Richter reading
14 Dept. boss
15 Silly behaviour
16 "The ___ Near!" (doomsayer's sign)
17 Fury
18 Termite's yearning?
20 *The National* time
22 Tend to the salad again
23 Whispered words
25 ___ B'rith
26 151, in Old Rome
29 Auburn hair tint
31 Kids' card game
33 America's 27th president
35 Three, in Torino
37 "Goodness gracious"
38 Bay window
40 Market place on Bay St.?
42 Brown ink
43 Be a traitor
45 Article in *Le Devoir*?
47 Retired Atl. fliers
48 Horse-drawn sleighs
50 Cube dimension
52 Choice word
53 Guzzle
55 There are 2 in 100
58 Mimic
60 Like a sedan
61 Negligent high-fibre muffin makers?
65 Scads, with "a"
66 Able was ___ saw . . .
67 China's Zhou ___
68 List catch-all
69 Ship's petty officer
70 Allied conference site, 1945
71 Like some phone nos.

DOWN

1 Leaves out
2 Jibe (with)
3 Where there's smoke, in Québec?
4 RCMP officers, e.g.
5 Egotist's numero?
6 "Like ___ not . . ."
7 Half of a record
8 Chequebook info.
9 Postcard scenes, often
10 Postie's load: Abbr.
11 Uganda's Amin
12 Employee ID
13 No ___ (menu boast)
19 Dahl of kids' fiction
21 Act
24 Explosive letters
26 Marksman who preys on freshwater fish?
27 "The sky's the ___!"
28 Brainstormers' output
30 Former Toronto mayor Eggleton
32 One who knows the score?
33 Hotsy ___
34 Not as ___ (rarely)
36 New Canadian's course: Abbr.
39 Woodsy retreat
41 Crossed (out)
44 Indira Gandhi's father
46 "Oh yeah? ___ who?"
49 Vancouver suburb
51 Iran, formerly
54 Intend to, slangily
56 Overact
57 Beats, to the band
58 Prefix meaning "air" or "wind"
59 Spill the beans
61 Baby's dinner wear
62 Model T contemporary
63 "___ Poetica" (Horace poem)
64 Fink

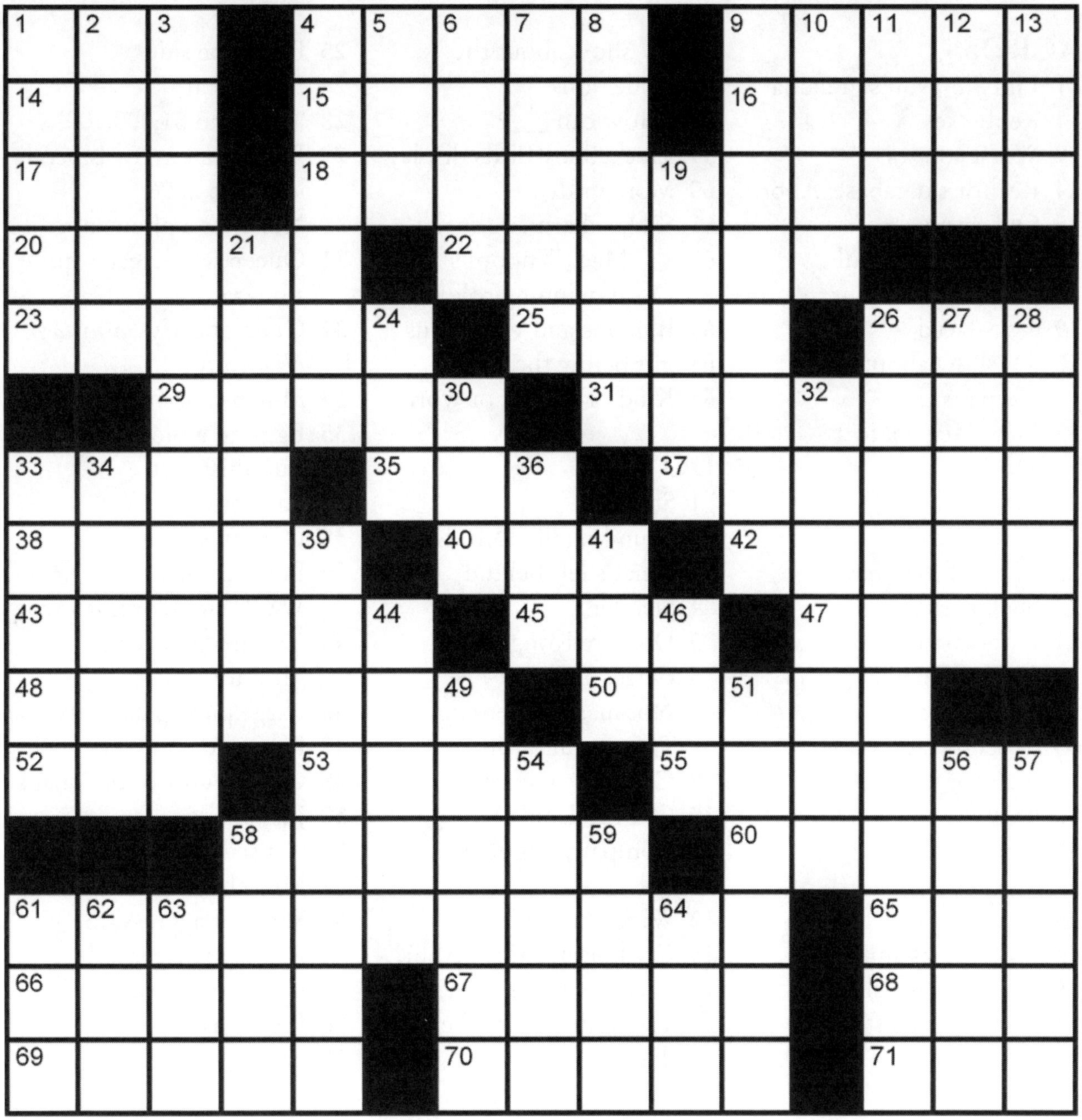

52 *All in the Family*

ACROSS

1 Lisa Simpson's grandpa
4 Rephrase
9 Weasel out of
14 Realtor's database: Abbr.
15 Old carnival act
16 The ___ Spoonful
17 Flatters for favour
19 Two-faced
20 TV show about the Cleavers
22 New Mexico, to a Mexican
23 Told all
24 Not natural
25 River of Flanders
27 Shamrock isle
31 Hors d'oeuvre cheese
33 Hall of Fame Dodgers' pitcher Sandy
35 TV show about the Nelsons
40 Swerved
41 Comic Johnson
42 "___ Love Her" (Beatles)
43 Grandma nicknames
45 It often has shingles
49 Monocle, for short
51 Earth pigment
53 TV show about the Andersons
58 "How can ___?"
59 Like a Snowbirds display
60 More miffed
61 Snake charmer's snake
62 ___ Mae (Whoopi's Oscar-winning role)
63 Bluefins and yellowfins
64 Hit below the belt?
65 Kind of weight or worth

DOWN

1 Strolled
2 Sounding like B.B. King
3 What's left behind
4 Slender as ___
5 Donkey Kong hero
6 Once, once
7 Not masc. or fem.
8 Throw out of office
9 Comic DeGeneres
10 Old Hudson's Bay Company supplier
11 Tel ___
12 Wine partner
13 Civil or electrical: Abbr.
18 Sitcom interruption
21 Try to drive off, like a dog
25 Feminine side
26 Family car
28 "___ Had $1,000,000"
29 Bob who ran for Liberal leader in 2006
30 No. after a phone no.
31 Queen who creates quite a buzz?
32 Gilda of early *Saturday Night Live*
34 Mined-over matter
35 Eggs, to a biologist
36 Buddhist sect
37 Last letter
38 Dublin is on it
39 Lots of mins.
44 WWII fighter pilot's woe
45 Country music's McEntire
46 Large pickup capacity
47 Behind the line in hockey
48 Contributor of big bucks
50 Jury makeup
51 Caused a bleep
52 Misbehaves
53 Show of aggression
54 Expos manager Felipe
55 Unable to decide
56 Light gas
57 Eat ___ eaten

53 *Get a Clue*

ACROSS

1 Jeep maker, once: Abbr.
4 Acts like a junkyard dog
10 Individually
14 Bad stuff in cigarettes
15 Ankle biter
16 Rolling "bones"
17 It's mined and refined
18 Fizzify
19 Other than this
20 Tool used in making tricky crossword clues
23 One who looks like hell, but is tempting?
24 Clark who wore super underwear
25 Word with dish or piano
28 Razz
31 Be rude, in a way
33 Whip
39 Aid and ___
40 Tool used in solving tricky crossword clues
42 ___ about (roughly)
43 Must
44 Latin dance music
46 Physical start
47 Part of RSVP
48 Picnic refreshments
52 Crashes, with "out"
56 Instant when a tricky crossword clue is solved
59 Brush (up)
62 Shredding gadget
63 Mad Hatter's drink
64 Comment after the fog clears
65 Not moving
66 Escort's offering
67 Blessing
68 Modern "alas"
69 Take a bough

DOWN

1 They split when they're smashed
2 *West Side Story* song
3 Toothpaste name
4 Like pear flesh, compared to that of apples
5 Regretful one
6 Fairy-tale fiend
7 Partner of ruin
8 Drink with a foamy top
9 Oktoberfest vessel
10 First place?
11 Feel under the weather
12 IV units
13 Start of a bray
21 They come from angry eyes
22 Late NHL periods
25 Way more than fervent
26 "Looks ___ everything"
27 Beginning, so to speak
29 Insipid
30 Scat woman
32 Draw a bead on
33 Dentist's direction
34 Island west of Maui
35 Lagoon area
36 Knobby-tired ride: Abbr.
37 The enemy
38 ___ *Kleine Nachtmusik* (Mozart serenade)
41 Assets minus liabilities
45 Spa sound
49 French painter of ballet scenes
50 Mother ___ News
51 Divvy up
53 Corolla component
54 Summer month in Montevideo
55 It may make an impression
56 It follows four or six, but not five
57 Suit to ___
58 Dinner in the corps
59 Lobsterfest necessity
60 Spanish bear
61 Prefix with natal

54 *Stressing Out!*

ACROSS

1 Green vehicles
6 Some can openers
10 Dancer's move
14 Once more
15 Work without ___
16 "Here comes trouble"
17 Jim's co-star in *Me, Myself and Irene*
18 Bitty lead-in
19 Darn
20 Tests for future hypnotists?
23 Tokyo, once
24 Bowie of baseball
25 Le déjeuner, for one
28 Songstress Mouskouri
30 Microscopic oriental side dish?
33 Neighbour of Syr.
35 Blind as ___
36 Supped
37 Tranquilizes
41 Fooled (around)
43 Mr. Onassis, briefly
44 Villa d'___ (Italian resort)
46 US campground
47 Abandon lab animals?
50 Pollution Probe concern
54 Wan
55 Coke ad word
57 Once ___ lifetime
58 Demonstrate verb forms?
62 Oolong alternative
64 Done with
65 Wart-causers of lore
66 Canadian red ___ (conifer)
67 Org. that's out of this world?
68 Move a tad
69 "Back in the ___" (Beatles)
70 Laryngitis MDs
71 Wrapped up

DOWN

1 Lurch dangerously
2 Meeting handout
3 Rave endlessly
4 Stadium level
5 Walk on tiptoe
6 Chinese martial art
7 TV's rabbit ear
8 ___ noire
9 Achilles soaker
10 Teacher's break
11 Stratford performer
12 Big time
13 Third degree?
21 Least sensitive
22 "Am not!" retort
26 Entr'___ (intermission)
27 Court rating
29 In the style of
31 Vancouver campus
32 Speaks without feedback
34 Fore'er
37 *Family* mom Thompson
38 "___ Tu" ('74 tune)
39 Sudsy basins
40 Juan de Fuca or Hudson, e.g.
42 Is in the past?
45 Seriously dedicated
48 More spine-tingling
49 Flashy fish
51 Make sum errors?
52 Like a recent non-smoker, say
53 ___ up (got fuel)
56 Leave alone
59 Sound unit
60 John's Welsh name
61 Proper part of speech
62 Computer's "grey matter": Abbr.
63 Brief greetings

55 *Vowel Play*

ACROSS

1 Oven liner
5 Pod veggies
9 Make joyful
14 Be rude, in a way
16 Island off Vancouver
17 He's married to Blondie
19 "Double Fantasy" singer
20 ___ -cone
21 Scale notes
22 University goal for some
28 Delhi attire
31 Small batt. size
32 Large shoe width
33 Hallowe'en colour
36 Reacted in fright
40 Enjoying a beatnik's party
42 Perform perfectly
43 Narc's target
44 Hockey's Tikkanen
45 $200 Monopoly props.
47 Violins and violas: Abbr.
48 Quaint tragedy
54 K-O fill
55 Building add-on
56 Ready, ___ , go!
59 Got into trouble
65 Early name in home computers
66 Lines of cliffs
67 ___ breath (delicate flower)
68 Melt together
69 Bank beavers don't make them

DOWN

1 Pal of Rover and Spot
2 ___ even keel
3 "Let ___" ("Quit worrying")
4 Kareem's original first name
5 Pitchfork feature
6 Popular email program
7 Police alert: Abbr.
8 Apt name for a cook?
9 Jed Clampett portrayer Buddy
10 "___ luck!"
11 Leave dumbstruck
12 Herbal soother
13 Terminus
15 House of York symbol
18 Modern medical scan: Abbr.
22 Aussie wild dog
23 Spring celebrations
24 Individually
25 Apply more salt, perhaps
26 Mall rat, usually
27 Passover meals
28 Laid new lawn
29 Melodic composition
30 Shabby
34 Actress Scala of *The Guns of Navarone*
35 Tolkien tree creature
37 Bad bottom-line colour
38 Ending with Siam or Japan
39 Make ___ for (justify)
41 *Chicago* star (2002)
46 Pays (out)
49 Magnificence
50 Old Dodge cars
51 Dir. from Halifax to Truro
52 Philanderer in a Michael Caine film (1966)
53 Provincial reps.
56 Designated driver's drink
57 Type of sch.
58 Dick Tracy's Trueheart
59 Apply lightly
60 Hagen of stage and screen
61 Chitchat
62 Abbr. on a lotion bottle
63 Perrier, to Pierre
64 "I've been ___!"

56 *Boo!*

ACROSS

1 Not overt, as a hint
7 "___ pronounce you . . ."
11 180° from NNW
14 Saw eye to eye
15 Nightclub in a Manilow tune
16 Columnist Abby's twin sister
17 Spooky scribe?
19 Battering ___
20 Newborn stats.
21 Unknown writer: Abbr.
22 Secretary's "about"
23 Ages and ages
25 '50s Conservative "Chief"
26 Quarter back?
27 SNL airer
28 Ghoulish show starring Alan Alda?
30 Baby talk
32 Car with bench seats
33 Dog biscuits, say
35 Capital of Cyprus
39 Sends e-junk
41 Irish game hunter
42 Broom Hilda's physician?
46 Environmentally friendly letters
47 "___ a dark and stormy night"
48 Small mountain lake
49 Peace signs
50 Cut for the grill
51 No ___ road
52 Spanish aunt
53 Spectra maker
54 Graveyard dweller's gate opener?
58 Env. insertion
59 Read intently, with "over"
60 Give consent
61 Roy Thomson Hall purchase: Abbr.
62 Gofer, say: Abbr.
63 Place to go downhill

DOWN

1 Aren't taut
2 "Yecch!"
3 Drink with Kahlua and milk
4 Samples
5 "Why don't we!"
6 Namesake of an Atlantic province: Abbr.
7 Bitter chill
8 Occasionally
9 Business sign
10 Card game that can last forever
11 Kim Mitchell's birthplace
12 Causes of much hair-tearing
13 Catch in a net
18 Ballgame downer
22 "You are so" retort
23 Grad given an iron ring: Abbr.
24 Radio letter between Nan and Peter
25 Thingamajig
26 Art class cheater
28 Undergoes a change
29 Hearing-impaired inventor
31 Tank top?
34 Suffocates
36 '70s fad follower
37 "Able was ___ . . ."
38 Pearson postings: Abbr.
40 Pimpernel colour
42 Croquet arch
43 Descartes' "cogito"
44 Like Beckett's play, *Waiting for Godot*
45 ___ *Lies* (Schwarzenegger film)
49 TV's Dominic Da ___
51 Boxing downers?
52 Clock sound
54 One place to get a face mask
55 Classroom helpers: Abbr.
56 Student's URL ending
57 Yearning

57 Vowel Play 2

ACROSS

1 Car battery brand
6 Flavourful
11 Get a lode of this
14 Cool and detached
15 "The First Time ___ Saw Your Face"
16 Tailor's concern
17 Scalawag's repertoire
19 Pub quaff
20 Cone or Cat preceder
21 "Je ne ___ pas"
22 Burning piles
24 Say "uncle," and then some
27 Attacked
30 They pop at high elevation
31 Muscat's land
32 ". . . or so ___!"
35 Flow's counterpart
38 Typical ad claim
41 Sound after a puncture
42 Rudy who sang through a megaphone
43 Sicilian erupter
44 Hand at a hacienda
45 Peanuts, essentially
46 Getting stuck, as in mud
51 Vice follower
52 "What's Hecuba to him ___ to Hecuba?": Hamlet
53 Fashion initials

56 Fourth periods in hockey
57 Scott Baio character in a 1976 kiddie musical
61 Abu Dhabi is its cap.
62 By land ___
63 Some frat party wear
64 Kazakhstan, once: Abbr.
65 Baptism et al.
66 Daytime TV fare

DOWN

1 Applies gently
2 Dashing style
3 Playboy bunny, for one
4 Sound like a pigeon
5 Printing method
6 Letter adornment
7 Dispatch boat
8 Push-up muscle
9 Annoy
10 Spread out
11 Saint Joan ___
12 Live the life of ___ (have it easy)
13 Dog days in Drummondville
18 "It" game
23 No. of candles on a cake, e.g.
24 Big ___ theory
25 The Cloister and the Hearth author Charles
26 Perhaps

27 Rips off
28 Friends of Frontenac
29 Henpecks
32 Persian, today
33 Raptor's weapon
34 Comedy revue since '75
35 Kitchen add-on
36 Big ___ Highway of the Columbia River
37 Some were burned in the '60s
39 Green Acres star
40 Many a mall rat
44 British sports cars
45 Gym wear
46 Computer test programs
47 Brian who skated to Olympic silver twice
48 "Have a look over there"
49 ___ a bone
50 Measure of resistance
51 S'il ___ plaît
53 It may put you in a difficult position
54 Ginger cookie
55 Not so much
58 Psychic Geller
59 Ottawa's six-percent solution: Abbr.
60 Head of England?

1	2	3	4	5		6	7	8	9	10		11	12	13
14						15						16		
17					18							19		
20				21						22	23			
			24					25	26					
27	28	29						30						
31					32	33	34					35	36	37
38				39							40			
41				42							43			
			44							45				
	46	47					48	49	50					
51							52					53	54	55
56				57	58	59					60			
61				62						63				
64				65						66				

58 *Sweep!*

ACROSS

1 Part of a written exam
6 CD add-on
9 Lady of Black
14 Arrest
16 Something between neighbours
17 Where Céline Dion might be heard
19 *Men in Black* extras
20 Comb-over alternative
21 What's left
22 Town council mem.
23 Tai ___
25 Drive-thru dinner choice
33 Rani wrap
34 Forward surge
35 180° from WNW
36 E.D. Smith competitor
38 Prefix meaning "self"
39 Japanese port
41 Blood-typing letters
42 ___ de corps
45 Part of CPU
46 Emotionally charged subject
49 Bush land?
50 Constituency reps
51 Rise dramatically, as prices
54 Drool
58 Hold up
61 Emulate elopers
64 Calgary Stampede event
65 Follows
66 Timetables, for short
67 Aries' season: Abbr.
68 C-3PO, for one

DOWN

1 Life of Riley
2 "Cuppa" quantity
3 Sunblock stats
4 It follows thou
5 Dr. Seuss's turtle
6 Received, in Québec
7 Like a Private potato peeler
8 Retailer's goods: Abbr.
9 Detective's cry
10 System adopted by Canada in 1970
11 "18 Til ___" (Bryan Adams)
12 Celebrity drivers?
13 Fast time
15 Rock formation seen near Radium, BC
18 PC pros
22 Similar (to)
24 Certain septet's refrain
25 Karate cousin
26 "What ___!" ("How fun!")
27 Not likely (to)
28 Town in eastern Nova Scotia
29 Took over a dance
30 Canadian actor Reeves
31 Edmonton CFLer, for short
32 Sans rocks
33 Iranian king, once
37 Mount Olympus bigwig
40 Investigate, with "out"
43 Sniffer dog's find
44 Finishline figures
47 Patted a baby, say
48 Vast estate
51 Eurasian divs., once
52 "Alright already!"
53 Right-hand man
55 Arachnid's octet
56 Rent-___ (security guard)
57 Shoot off-course
58 Prefix with "tiller"
59 "The ___ Love" (R.E.M. song)
60 Polar explorer Richard
62 How-___ (do-it-yourselfer's tips)
63 Product maker: Abbr.

■ BARBARA OLSON

59 *A Chilling Deduction*

ACROSS

1 Tartan's representation
5 Amer. military fliers
9 "Dreamboat Annie" band
14 Like smoked oysters
15 Prefix meaning "equal"
16 Boredom in French class?
17 Press people
19 Escorted from outside
20 Start of a quip
22 Neighbour of Leb.
23 ___ Kong
24 Beaver baby
27 Macdonald's bills
30 Degree of flexibility
34 More of the quip
37 Rock diva Turner
38 ___ Penh
39 High craggy hill
40 Help in French class?
41 Piñata whacker's no-no
42 The quip continues . . .
44 Show up
46 Salt shake
47 *Rushmore* director Anderson
48 Removes tears carefully
50 MDs' milieux
52 End of the quip

59 Role for Jenny Lind
60 Little bear in the sky
61 Founder of the Grand River Reserve
62 Swimmers' race
63 "___ help you?"
64 Beetle Bailey's boss
65 Priest's title in Québec
66 Gordian or Windsor

DOWN

1 Cola opener
2 Neeson of the screen
3 Town near the Saguenay River
4 Trotskian turndowns
5 In trouble, bigtime
6 "Ditto"
7 Carpet layer's measurement
8 Certain seedeater
9 *Chez* ___ (early children's TV show)
10 Vivacious
11 Me, myself, ___
12 Wrack's mate
13 Sn in chemistry
18 Beat in the band
21 Ship's storage area

24 Tenth Greek letter
25 "Devil ___ Heart" (Beatles)
26 Stereo component
28 Western defence grp.
29 Prepared to sing "O Canada"
31 Black ___ (deadly arachnid)
32 Anoint ceremoniously
33 Eskimos' gains
35 "I'm serious!"
36 Columnist Bombeck
40 Guru's getaway
42 Country's McEntire
43 Keep separate
45 Head out
49 Slow time on Bay Street
51 Ballpoint alternative
52 Mystical glow
53 Raleigh's state: Abbr.
54 Early Manitoban
55 Lousy friend, usually
56 ___ instant (pronto)
57 Taboo
58 Trudeau or Turner, informally
59 There are two in 908 gms.

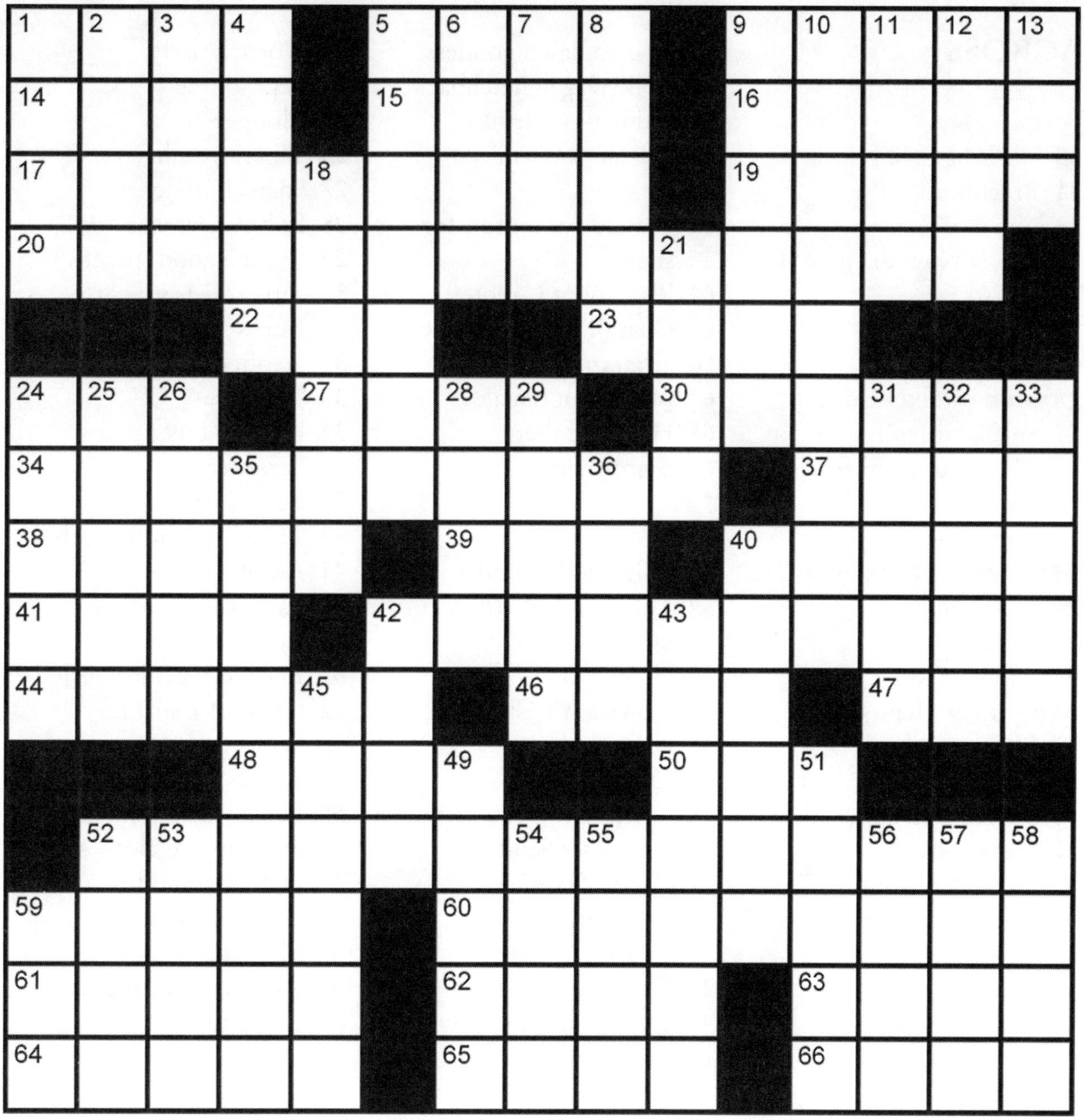

60 *On the Sly*

ACROSS

1 "___ out?" (dealer's query)
5 Walking on air
11 Blockhead
14 Not any
15 Olivia Newton-John flick (1980)
16 Yoko ___
17 Brother of Cain
18 Moon walker Buzz
19 Suffix with schnozz
20 The Road Runner bugs him
22 Ran into
23 First king of England
24 Casa room
26 Mishmash
31 Simpson kid
33 Prefix with physics
37 Singer Guthrie
38 "Yes ___ ?"
39 Dickens pickpocket
42 Ages and ages
43 "Think nothing ___"
44 Like an unkempt lawn
45 Vegan's no-no
46 Fame
48 Lasting impression?
50 Roman dawn goddess
55 Volkswagen hatchback
56 Kahlua-rye drinks
61 Tic-tac-toe win
62 Chaste
63 Muscle-car motor, for short
64 Play about Capote
65 Coat on bronze statues
66 Saharan
67 Males, not females
68 Here and there
69 Light snack

DOWN

1 Filled with wonder
2 "It's ___ deal" (don't worry)
3 Sixteen ozs.
4 US Grant's Civil War adversary
5 Quinella kin
6 *Mission: Impossible* theme composer Schifrin
7 Capp of comics
8 Poi source
9 Polish writing
10 Desert sights
11 Impend in a big way
12 Not scholarly
13 Feta source
21 Blooper
25 Where you live
27 Social blunder
28 Bobby Orr was one
29 ___ the good (peachy)
30 Title role for George Burns
32 Stephen Harper is one
33 "Lemme ___!"
34 Place to buy pumps
35 Persistent
36 Bob Marley was one
40 "The Big Smoke": Abbr.
41 Admit (to)
47 Attack from behind
49 Replies to a host
51 Recovery project, briefly
52 Cheri of *Liar Liar*
53 Word on an invoice
54 Words to the audience
55 Person who wears dark makeup and clothes
57 Half-moon tide
58 This, in Tijuana
59 Plugging away
60 German philosopher Immanuel

61 *Food for Thought*

ACROSS

1 It's often autographed
5 With 65-Across, these are low in 35-Across
10 Rock equipment
14 Eight, in combos
15 Melee
16 Drain slowly
17 Big shoe seller Thom
18 Races in a harness
19 Part of EMT: Abbr.
20 Typical drive-thru lunch
23 ___ Martin (James Bond sports car)
24 Vitamin bottle: Abbr.
25 Stephen of *The Crying Game*
26 Your: Fr.
27 Give the slip
31 Freaky
33 Have ___ to play
34 Northern BC river of the Nisga'a
35 Reputed health hazard in 20- and 53-Across
39 Certain
41 They have strings attached
42 Checkout count
44 Tree that's yellow in fall
45 Freebie at some gas stations
48 Off-road transport: Abbr.
49 Boy who's a doll
51 Church donation
53 Two for dinner?
58 Hebrides tongue
59 Pilotless plane
60 "I ___ my wit's end!"
61 Zaire's Mobutu ___ Seko
62 Like Poe's prose
63 Fomer capital of Italy
64 Land west of Nod
65 See 5-Across
66 Whole lot

DOWN

1 Activity of war
2 Lay blame
3 Is on the first team
4 To dance in Argentina
5 Science studying galaxies: Abbr.
6 Feudal farmhand
7 "Do ___ else!"
8 Garb
9 Barely won, with "out"
10 Not long to wait
11 It's often carved in stone
12 Cheaters of a sort
13 Ranches, familiarly
21 First page of el calendario
22 One going back and forth to work
28 Encyclopedia unit: Abbr.
29 It has a head and hops
30 Pupils' places
32 Cain's nephew
33 Attention getter
35 Glacier feature
36 It comes to those who wait
37 Québec's Festival d'___
38 Start to car or cop
39 Kind of cat or twin
40 Put into words
43 Reggae relative
44 Soviet Cold War diplomat Gromyko
45 Age beginning in the '40s
46 "___ Symphony" (Supremes hit)
47 Took it easy
50 Broke off
52 Tilted letters, for short
54 *Dawson's Creek* extra
55 Hole in the skin
56 Words after sleep or step
57 Tiger's pocketful

62 *Tons of Fun*

ACROSS

1 Composter's buy
6 Chip in china, say
10 Leaking wet goo
14 Crazy as ___
15 Like Lucille Ball
17 Certain NDPer's travel arrangements?
19 Lion tamer's item
20 Bill's added amts.
21 Deteriorates bigtime
25 Business bldg.
28 Frequent joiner
29 Midwife's announcement on December 25, 1642?
33 Oliver's lunch
36 Winter driving needs
37 ___ the hole
39 Big-mouthed pitchers
40 Most sickeningly slick
44 Letter-shaped bolt holders
46 Depending on Dolly's decision?
48 Mideast grp.
49 Legal conclusion?
50 Like modern factories
53 Salon jobs
56 Hertz rival
57 Yo-yo trick performed by a marine biologist?
64 Kept aside for later
65 "Toodle-oo!"
66 It's passed in class
67 Founded: Abbr.
68 *Love Story* author Erich

DOWN

1 ___-Mart
2 Cray or pay ending
3 ___ Thomson Hall
4 Light fixtures?
5 Haughty type
6 Fruity drinks over shaved ice
7 1960s US poet Welch
8 Get comfortable with
9 Kids' questions, often
10 Renoir's supplies
11 ___ pro nobis
12 Buddhist path to enlightenment
13 Eskimos' meas.
16 Fitting
18 When the clock strikes twelve
21 Kind of order
22 Freeway entrances
23 Instructor's aim
24 Lease-to-___
25 Infected or impure
26 Train bridge
27 Patient people?: Abbr.
30 Are outstanding
31 Pkg. info
32 "Ça va ___"
34 Finnish architect Saarinen
35 Have a bum leg
38 Actress Vardalos
40 *Talking Sex with ___*
41 Pencil case items
42 McLean of *The Vinyl Café*, to friends
43 Came to, in Tennessee
45 Greenskeeper's turf
47 Super star?
51 Compact cars
52 "Don't ___" (shrugger's words)
53 ___-Ball (arcade game)
54 French connections?
55 It was you once
57 Take home the Stanley Cup, say
58 Year, to Juan
59 Commuter train syst.
60 New soldier: Abbr.
61 Clothe
62 Son-gun link
63 Super Bowl org.

■ DAVE MACLEOD

63 *Focus on Solvers*

ACROSS
1 Taco belles?: Abbr.
6 "Git!"
11 Selkirks and Laurentians: Abbr.
14 Canadian capital?
15 Vincent of horror flicks
16 Thick ___ brick
17 Weasel out of
18 Chopper blade
19 Where the Stars play the Blues
20 First follow-up
22 It's Big in California
23 Testy state
24 Solver's problematic situation
27 Rights, casually
30 St. Bernard feature
31 Like sour grapes
32 Spanish bear
33 Kind of shark
34 Highway hauler
35 Solver's challengers
40 Half of Mork's greeting
41 Shower affection
42 China's Chairman
43 PMs, e.g.
44 Full of pep
45 Nile goddess

46 Solver's bane
49 On guard
50 With 45-Down, "How come?" comeback
51 Whistler event in the 2010 Olympics
55 Confrère
56 Pokémon cards, e.g.
58 Two-faced
59 Dundee denial
60 String quartet instrument
61 Gravelly glacial ridge
62 Ninny
63 Monica of tennis
64 Christmas songs

DOWN
1 Cows and sows
2 All-night bash
3 ___ II (razor brand)
4 Peripherals
5 Play thing
6 It starts in Mar.
7 Solver's raison d'être
8 Mass, for one
9 Nut with a cap
10 Debussy's "La ___"
11 Quirks
12 Casual cover-up
13 Preserves, in a way

21 Eerie feeling
23 Hindu teacher
25 Okey-___
26 Remembrance Day monument: Var.
27 Grumpy's cohort
28 Mideast map: Abbr.
29 Fences
33 Capital of Belarus
34 Lacivious goat-men of myth
36 Sideshow worker
37 When doubled, an island near Tahiti
38 Mai ___
39 Plea at sea
43 Andes pack animals
44 Sudden storm
45 See 50-Across
46 *Call Me* ___ (1963 Hope film)
47 Mountainside debris
48 Sigourney's role in *Alien*
52 Word often heard from teens
53 1977 Scott Turow book
54 Baseball VIPs
56 IV units
57 Dawn goddess

■ BARBARA OLSON

64 *Two in One*

ACROSS

1 "Hosers" show
5 Flaky rock
10 "___ to end all . . ." (Woodrow Wilson)
14 *The Time Machine* people
15 Wished
16 Actress Ward of *Sisters*
17 Place for a float
18 Heart part
19 Beauty buff's mag
20 Recount "Hansel and Gretel"?
23 Wee hour
24 Keg brew
25 Osgoode Hall outputs: Abbr.
27 Juan de Fuca, e.g.
28 "Yuck!"
30 Morsel
32 Hugs in writing
33 Ont. classical grp.
34 Go a-courting?
35 Altar words
36 Apprehend actor Brad?
40 Berserk
41 ___ out (happen)
42 Sawmiller's union: Abbr.
43 Traveller's info.
44 French fire

45 "Golly"
46 Wee, to Burns
49 Leaf's pore
51 "B-I-___ . . ." (kids' song)
53 Introduction to alcohol?
55 Help steal one of Emily's paintings?
58 Course of action
59 Bawl out
60 Burn remedy
61 Sask.'s neighbour
62 Prefix meaning "sun"
63 Welsh actor Novello
64 Part of DOS: Abbr.
65 Snaky moves
66 Prepares the table

DOWN

1 Skirmishes
2 Marketer's coup
3 Cranston on ice
4 Country estate
5 It was underfoot in the '70s
6 "Yippie!"
7 Spring-ahead month
8 Jailbird's cry, maybe
9 Cheese choice
10 Take ___ (sit down)

11 Financially set
12 Comic character from Moo
13 Actress Charlotte of *Diff'rent Strokes*
21 Tickle
22 Make lace
26 Help, at sea
29 Cut loose
31 Knot again
33 Ringside ruling
34 Employee ID
35 "Isn't ___ pity?"
36 In a fatal way
37 Those in high places
38 Pot bellies
39 "Neat," to some
40 ___ Palmas
44 Dieter's bane
45 Hockey's Howe
46 Abandon for now
47 "Baloney!"
48 Takes in or out
50 ___ Work (Aussie band)
52 Actress O'Grady and runner Devers
54 Bangkok natives
56 Tylenol target
57 Classic cars
58 N'est-ce ___?

65 *Feeling Grand*

ACROSS

1 Plugging away
5 ___ luxury
10 "Venerable" English saint
14 Motown's Diana
15 Ryan or Tatum
16 The very top
17 ___ Bora (Afghan region)
18 Brief brawl
19 PDQ
20 Grand, in an imposing way
23 West of old Hollywood
24 Beseeches
25 Author Deighton
26 Book of maps
28 Fairway clubs
30 2003 Masters champ Mike
31 Good judgment
36 Too grand
38 Giant squid, to Captain Nemo
41 *Othello* villain
45 Acquired relative
46 Wing it
47 Iceland's ocean: Abbr.
48 They're not up for Oscars
54 It can see through any body: Abbr.

55 Having delusions of grandeur
58 Cupid's Greek counterpart
59 Left-hand page
60 School course part
62 Mailed away
63 Data addition
64 Lie in the sun
65 River to Kassel, Germany
66 Debussy duet?
67 Bounce off the walls

DOWN

1 Pop or Dada
2 Past the deadline
3 Haifa resident
4 Former despot: Var.
5 "I'm a ___" (Beatles song)
6 End of ___
7 Piddling
8 They're taken on a stand
9 Parade attraction
10 Jezebel's deity
11 Fifth Greek letter
12 Makes way too much 22-Down
13 It's often deductible
21 Family docs

22 Din
23 It's usually gaping
27 Bakery come-on
29 Updated, perhaps
31 Chick's mom
32 IV sites
33 Queue after Q
34 "Sprechen ___ Deutsch?"
35 Book before Neh.
37 *Wheel of Fortune* buy
38 Kind of cat or twin
39 Popped in
40 Not available anymore
42 Handy desk reference
43 Feminine
44 Japanese wraparound
46 Hard ___ rock
49 Kind of theatre
50 Eclipses, to some
51 Rain-delay rollouts
52 Come next
53 Runs amok
56 Science of stars: Abbr.
57 3-D square
61 Ring decision, for short

■ BARBARA OLSON

66 *The Walloping Gourmet*

ACROSS

1 Topics on *Oprah*
6 Red state?
9 "You ___ mouthful!"
14 The Walloping Gourmet's soufflé mixer
16 Poet Pound, and others
17 Blabbermouth's trait
18 Crete's highest peak
19 It's done in Québec
20 Attaches, as a ribbon
21 The Walloping Gourmet's tropical drink
26 "He's making ___ , checking . . ."
27 Responsibility
28 To-do list item
29 Bounced off the walls?
32 A language of Thailand
35 The Walloping Gourmet's cookie-making step
38 Letters on a bow
39 Capable kid's retort
40 David Suzuki's concern: Abbr.
41 Chowder morsel
42 Rust, e.g.
43 The Walloping Gourmet's bread spread
47 Member of Gretzky's team
49 Scratch off the list
50 Butler's belle
51 Reykjavik resident
56 Playful swimmer
57 The Walloping Gourmet's favourite meat
58 Pal of Richie and Ralph
59 Switch positions
60 Understood without words

DOWN

1 "Runaway" singer Shannon
2 "Where did ___ wrong?"
3 Id kin
4 Popular movie channel
5 Deem apt
6 Singer Turner's autobiography
7 Adjust the corsage, say
8 CPR stations?
9 Like a modest streaker
10 Early Mexicans
11 Brian Mulroney's lineage
12 Groove in wood
13 Stong ___ ox
15 Others, to Ovid
20 Lock the radio dial on
21 Concoct, as a plan
22 Burglar's foil
23 Gets smart, with "up"
24 ___ silly question . . .
25 Standard partner, in investment
29 Getaway, in a way
30 Blue ribbon winner
31 Part of the PM's title
32 Within the law
33 Jumper-cable connector
34 Stare case?
36 General interest?
37 Queue cue
41 Stable work
42 Surpass fellow auditioners
43 An Earp brother
44 Freed felon, for short
45 Busy bodies
46 Popular grocery-store section
47 Eggs' place, maybe
48 "___ be in England": Browning
51 Stk. market debut
52 Montréal Canadiens' early org.
53 Member of a fairy-tale septet
54 It may be left of centre?
55 They're behind U

67 * Empty Promises

ACROSS

1 Suit
6 Pod orb
9 Iranian cash
14 Type of acid
15 Musketeers' concern
16 Door word
17 Tam accompaniments
18 Successful inventors, usually
20 Scat woman
21 Scarlet ___ (bright bird)
22 Search's partner
24 * Fail to come up with an answer
26 That's a fact
28 What Costner did with wolves
31 "Steal My Sunshine" band
33 Airy areas
36 Exit
37 Secretariat's chow
39 * "%&$#@!!" (politely)
41 Not kosher: Var.
42 Poe's house name
44 Simmers
46 Take a stab at
47 Vacillate
49 American taste
51 * Zombie's look
54 Roper's rope

57 Snickers ingredient
59 Don't rev
60 Restless longing
63 Get started
64 Like old whiskey barrels, often
65 '90s hair stuff
66 Opt (with "to")
67 Sighs of relief
68 Oui in Outremont
69 Formula One curves

DOWN

1 Pie maker
2 Author Zola
3 * Answers a crossword clue
4 Undamaged
5 Fros partners
6 Hemingway sobriquet
7 African antelope
8 Sacrifice site
9 Subscriber's action
10 Corporate connections
11 Bothered (with "at")
12 Director Spike
13 They often get discounts: Abbr.
19 "Yikes!" once
21 * Paper handed out on exam day

23 Chant at the LA Olympics
25 * Starter-pistol ammo
27 Galena and cinnabar
29 ". . . happily ___ after."
30 Say no to
31 Oaf
32 Life of Riley characteristic
34 Addams Family cousin
35 Sailor's assents
38 Metal parts fastener
40 * Place for a mural
43 Keeps
45 Baden-Baden, e.g.
48 T-bone order
50 Bay windows
52 Gangly
53 Roast host
55 Dennis the Menace's mother
56 Goes camping
58 Morays, for instance
60 Wow lead-in
61 College cheer
62 Hilo guitar, for short
63 Spelling competition

* This puzzle, when completed, will still have some "unfinished business."

68 *What Lies Beneath*

ACROSS

1 Expressed relief, in a way
6 ___ Na Na
9 Hy's menu choice
14 Lemon orchard
15 Word with hat or dog
16 Jagged-edged, as a leaf
17 Happy as ___
18 Deviation from the norm
20 Sparring trainees
22 Old Spanish bread?
23 More upscale
27 Engine's cold water conveyor
31 Wit lead-in
34 Fishing or hunting need
35 Canadian singer Paul
36 Battery terminal
38 Fair hiring abbr.
39 Emotionless
40 "Sock ___ me, baby!"
41 Iqaluit cover-up
43 Receiving the CCP, e.g.
44 Verbal gaffe exposing hidden thoughts
47 Gloomy, south of 49
48 Hub of Ancient Greece
52 Slow developers
56 "Lost Together" band
59 Roman love goddess
60 Real looker
61 "A little ___'ll do ya!"
62 Beethoven's "Für ___"
63 Shampoo label boast
64 Grey Cupper's gains
65 Blows off some steam

DOWN

1 Utterly shocked
2 Prefix with -type, meaning "first"
3 Greetings in Granada
4 Tax auditor's target
5 Recording studio send-in
6 Crack, shot or whirl
7 Boxcar rider, maybe
8 Pinnacle
9 Extreme fear
10 Military bigwig
11 Cart follower?
12 US defence grp.
13 Bigfoot's shoe width, maybe
19 Tend to a houseplant, in a way
21 Use the kids' pool
24 Pay tribute to Americans?
25 Edmonton footballer, for short
26 Are not passive
28 "The Faerie Queene" character
29 "I'm being followed by ___ shadow . . ." (Cat Stevens lyric)
30 Cake layers
31 Innocent ones
32 Brief foreword?
33 Tribal pole
37 Share a twin bed, say
39 Omit
41 ___-surface missile
42 As well
45 Severe shortage
46 Wallin of talk TV
49 Kidney enzyme
50 "___ me, I know"
51 Bungling fools
53 Whirlpool
54 A bit of sweat
55 Some bird flights?
56 Barrel: Abbr.
57 Writer Tolstoy
58 GM employee's union, in US

69 *About Face*

ACROSS

1 "Why ___ I think of that!"
6 Yours, to Yves
10 Booty
14 "God ___ Refuge" (Mozart)
15 Muffin choice
16 Spicy dish, or its pot
17 Nevil who wrote *On the Beach*
18 Mix master
20 One who knows how to raise a few eyebrows?
22 Metal marble
23 Sue Grafton bestseller ___ *for Ricochet*
24 Comprehend
25 Lamebrain
30 Top-notch beef grade
33 Former Egyptian leader Anwar
35 Present opening
36 Words of a 20-Across after a day at work?
40 Actor with an Oskar role (1993)
41 ". . . woman who lived in ___"
42 Poker word
43 Sit on Silver
46 Alphabet run
48 Logical start
49 More portly
53 What a 20-Across is paid to do?
58 Poisonous mushroom
59 ___ crow flies
60 Jane Austen heroine
61 "Lean ___" (Withers tune)
62 It's small in Ste.-Foy
63 Broke down
64 In said order: Abbr.
65 Decree

DOWN

1 Frisbees and pie plates
2 "___ the Sheriff" (Eric Clapton)
3 Put out, as fire
4 Eggnog spice
5 Like a clearcut
6 American activist Hoffman
7 Gillette product, with "II"
8 They're what propelled Silken Laumann?
9 Successively
10 Slim chance
11 Shoppe descriptor, often
12 Parkay product
13 Small mountain lake
19 TV's Estrada
21 Atlas, for one
25 Memory gap
26 Mormon stronghold
27 Ostrich cousins
28 Suffix with annoy
29 Use sandbags
30 Feels feverish
31 Going ___ (bickering)
32 "___ to end all . . ." (Woodrow Wilson)
34 Dove rival
37 Blown away by
38 Nick of *The Deep*
39 Singer's send-in
44 Lower case letter toppers
45 Rx provider
47 Restored to health
49 Lug awkwardly: Var.
50 "___ Frutti"
51 Set of morals
52 Butler in a book
53 Crock-pot concoction
54 Heavy reading
55 Wheelchair access
56 Give an edge to
57 Cochrane and Connors

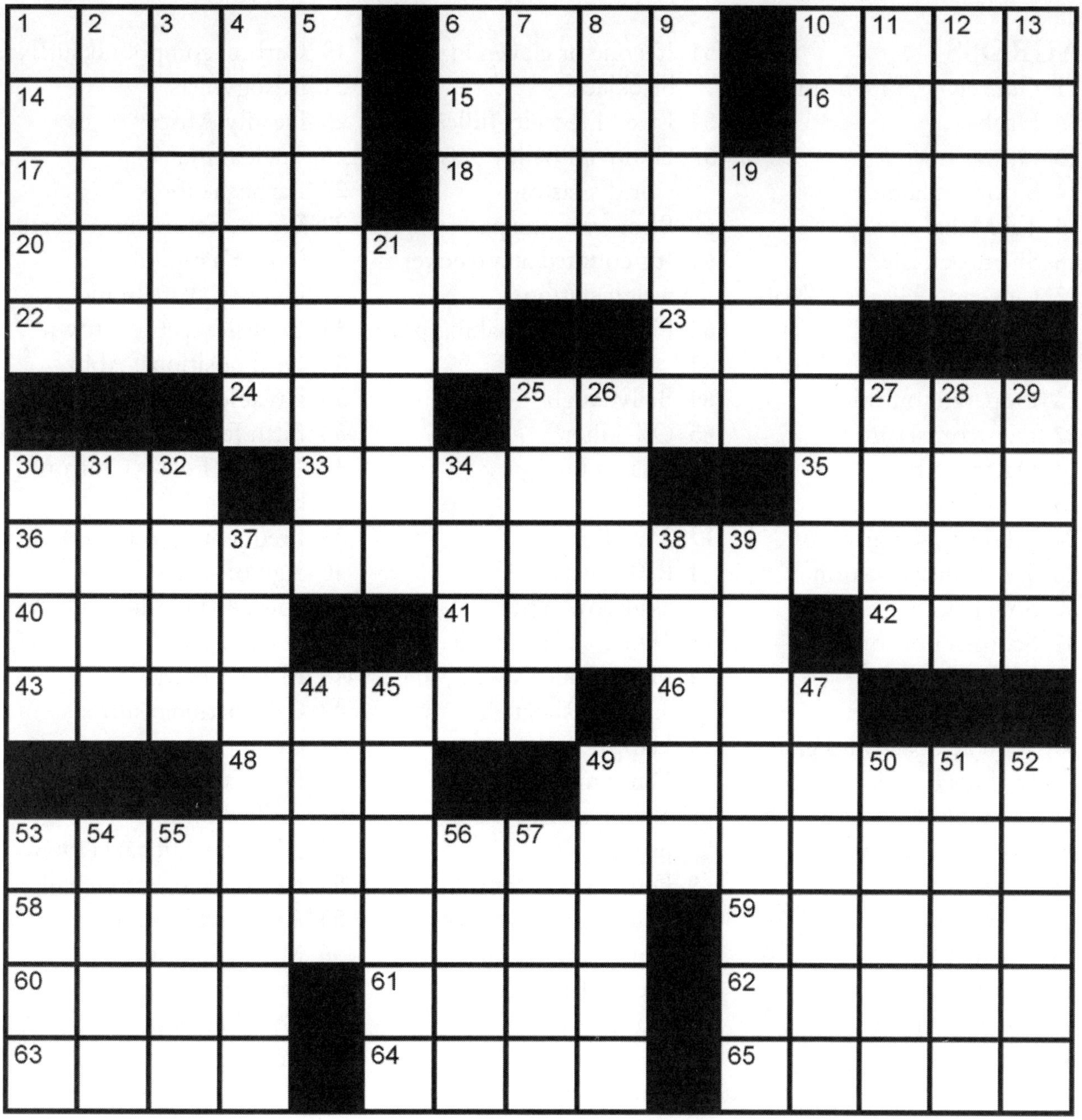

70 *Up for Grabs*

ACROSS

1 *Gulliver's Travels* author
6 Hacks
10 Di was one
14 Sir or madam
15 Taj Mahal city
16 Shamrock isle
17 One-time UN head Kofi ___
18 Traffic mishap
20 Prepared to testify
22 Dir. from Truro to Dartmouth
23 Stumblebum
24 NDPers, slangily
28 TV-dinner platform
30 Soul mate
31 Scottish port on the North Sea
36 Certain winner
39 Won at a backyard game for kids
41 Cantankerous sorts
42 React to a haymaker
43 Stutz Bearcat contemporary
44 Ancient kingdom near the Dead Sea
45 Large wardrobe
49 Kind of doll
51 It's one or eleven in blackjack
54 Lived life to its fullest
57 Donovan Bailey was the world's fastest
60 Blast from the past
61 It's counted at a trucker's weigh station
62 Plant used in making poi
63 ___ HOOKS
64 Belly laugh
65 Off-kilter
66 Osama bin ___

DOWN

1 RBIs and ERAs
2 Skid-row types
3 "Do ___!" (immediately)
4 Fighter pilot's woe
5 9:50, for short
6 Happy-go-lucky
7 Many moons
8 Young and spoiled, probably
9 Fergie's real name
10 Tennis great who never won Wimbledon
11 Word after legal or hearing
12 Dr. of rap
13 The Beatles' "___ Blues"
19 Carbon compound suffix
21 Misogynists
25 Deadly African virus
26 Tuck's title
27 Barbecue tools
29 Words before on or forth
31 Ghana's capital
32 Hockey skate brand
33 English racetrack town
34 Grid positions: Abbr.
35 Payable
36 Fifth Jewish month
37 "___ So Fine" (Chiffons hit)
38 Frequently, in verse
40 Sign of sorrow
44 Source of tequila and peyote: Var.
46 Blender brand
47 Occupational suffix
48 Cowboy's rope
50 Hallowe'en costume
51 Tacked on
52 *Alfie* star Michael (1966)
53 Keep one's ___ the ball
55 Architect Saarinen
56 Movie lioness
57 In the distance
58 Bouillon name
59 Ending with schnozz

■ BARBARA OLSON

71 *Whose What?*

ACROSS

1 Guy's girl
4 Butt of humour
9 Fill with dread
14 Kanga's kid
15 In-basket items, maybe
16 ___ time (soon enough)
17 Like some vbs.
18 Dickens boy's verbal "attitude"?
20 Hot time in Québec
21 The sail constellation
22 "Either you leave ___ will!"
23 Prosperity, slangily
25 Fix, as makeup
29 Lower digits
30 Homer and Marge
31 Finger-crossers, maybe
33 Become an ex
34 Is in the past?
35 Celtic tongue
36 Egg part
37 Pub projectile
38 European crow
39 Bavarian beverages
40 Companies
41 As one
43 Eloquent equine of old TV

44 City's fortress
45 "I dunno"
48 Logan and McKinley: Abbr.
49 Get what one deserves
50 Playground pastime
51 Poet Service's push-pin?
55 HS timetable word
56 Ordinary beginning?
57 ___ wool (abrasive pad)
58 Brazilian hot spot
59 Dull brownish
60 Use the tea towel again
61 Palindromic Bobbsey

DOWN

1 "Good ___!"
2 Major artery
3 Singer Lynn's clever repartee?
4 Not blockbusters
5 Takes on new tenants
6 Painter Carr
7 Super star
8 Bay St. trading hub
9 Cause a ruckus
10 Goofy behaviour
11 Ginseng kin
12 Sister to many
13 ___ up (arrange)

19 Dorm sharer, casually
24 Prepare pears
25 Isn't plumb
26 Billionaire Hughes's grey gull?
27 Render weaponless
28 Attention getters?
30 Pinnacled
31 City 30 kilometres south of Edmonton
32 Tehran native
33 Esso rival
36 Most expansive
37 Be a loser, maybe
39 Hospital meal table
40 Openly, as in speech
42 Whip-crackers
43 Maritime comedian Rick
45 Spoke sheepishly?
46 Frantic state
47 With ___ one's face
49 Diminutive ending
51 "Losing My Religion" band
52 Bovril shelfmate
53 Heat meas.
54 Bulgaria, once: Abbr.

72 *Chill Out*

ACROSS

1 Track event
5 General on a Chinese menu
8 Bring in from across the border
14 Whole bunch
15 Directly across from: Abbr.
16 Hang-glider
17 With 38-Across, when things get hectic . . .
20 List catch-all
21 More uncivil
22 ___ all-time low
23 Start to date?
25 Like beer from the tap
28 Attention
30 Was in session
33 Too too
34 "Easy!"
36 It can be active or passive
38 (17-Across continued . . .)
44 Unfamiliar with
45 Woods with clubs
46 Beachside bathhouse
50 High school subj.
52 Flirt crudely
53 Crossword solvers are often these, as well
55 Lit. compilation
57 Enemy or fiend preceder

58 Start of el año
61 It may be inflated
64 And once you've arrived at 38-Across . . .
68 Perpetual, in poems
69 It's faith-based: Abbr.
70 Ancient region bordering Palestine
71 Imperturbable
72 Price of a visit
73 Deflation indicator

DOWN

1 One-time BC MLA, now political commentator Mair
2 Touched down
3 How some chili is prepared
4 Trudeau airport listing: Abbr.
5 McKenzie Brothers' headwear
6 Stompin' Tom's comes from PEI
7 Mayberry boy
8 Loyal or royal follower
9 Unkempt hair
10 Royal residence
11 Eloquent speaker
12 Amnesiac's lack
13 All the rage

18 Gallery display
19 "___ tu" (Verdi aria)
24 Within earshot
26 ___-Cola
27 Woodstock was a big one
28 Cornfield call
29 Fire proof?
31 Declare openly
32 It's all in Montréal
35 Tubular alternative to bowties
37 Windows graphic
39 Time for a revolution?
40 Run amok
41 Really smart people
42 Poivre partner
43 Amount past due?
46 Orange containers
47 Make bubbly
48 Funder
49 Stick (to)
51 Mix up
54 "Get it?"
56 Easter preceder?
59 Soft ball
60 Fencing weapon
62 Sporty '60s Pontiacs
63 Resistance units
65 Raggedy doll
66 Poor grade
67 Really poor grades

73 *Yes, Yes, Yes!*

ACROSS

1 Pilgrimage place
6 Campus sight
10 Hoodwink
14 Pop star Lavigne
15 Seized car
16 Teen's bane
17 Betty Ford Center grad
19 Fork-tailed gull
20 Sailor's "yes"
22 Transatl. jet, once
24 Teacher's favourite
25 Spirit-raising event
26 "Slow Hand" sisters
29 Give advice
30 At ___ for words
31 One in Düsseldorf
32 Trucker's "yes"
40 San Francisco's ___ Hill
41 Sleep soundly?
42 Trellis pattern
47 Garfield's favourite food
49 Dancing round and round
50 Sept plus trois
51 Ont. hub
52 Ned Flanders' "yes"
56 Vocal quality
57 Whiners after a game
60 Plaintiff
61 Indigo-yielding plant
62 Preminger and others
63 Pearson or Trudeau letters
64 US department-store founder
65 Lake near Reno

DOWN

1 Mudroom item
2 It follows Christmas?
3 Big Bang alternative
4 Hamilton, Halifax or Hope
5 Lily extract
6 Talk in church
7 Rent out again
8 Crude grp.
9 At little expense
10 Wicker-like fibre
11 Clover Leaf rival
12 How to serve moo goo guy pan
13 Pooch's place
18 Record
21 Un ___ (a little, in Laval)
22 Tiff
23 Cobbler's concern
27 Cheque letters, maybe
28 Roy Thomson Hall grp.
29 102 in Old Rome
31 Back off at the beach
33 Finger-pointing poster man
34 Fish eggs
35 Stretches the truth
36 Actress Merkel
37 Canines and incisors
38 Bond baddie
39 Calendar span
42 Founder of Taoism
43 Invite to dinner, say
44 Twisted, in a way
45 Layers of flooring
46 Wrath
47 "Not ___!" ("As if!")
48 Leaf-stem angle
50 Not Ionic or Corinthian
53 Spanish title
54 Raid during a riot
55 "¿Cómo ___ usted?"
58 Milne marsupial
59 Dawson City–Whitehorse dir.

74 *Aah, Summertime!*

ACROSS

1 Gushing flattery
6 Swedish auto
10 Torso's lack
14 Lose one's cool
15 "That's ___!" (words from the accused)
16 Candidate's goal
17 "I Am ___" (Paul Simon)
18 Ore store
19 Murky
20 How you have it when 57-Across
23 Caterer's heater
24 Concerning
25 Neighbour of Leb.
27 It can be flipped
29 Summer drink
31 Pop singer Brickell
34 Part of NHLPA
37 Mineral abundant in oysters
38 State of affairs when 57-Across
41 Canal feature
42 Fitzgerald of scat
43 Word with candy or sugar
44 Home of 5-Down
46 Volkswagen hatchback
48 Filbert or pecan
49 Counterpart of Mars

52 Hindu retreat
57 Line in "Summertime" (*Porgy and Bess*)
60 Pinball sin
61 *Lives of the Saints* author Ricci
62 Do-___ situation
63 Blessing
64 Ambassador's gift
65 Prepared for action
66 The "I" of *The King and I*
67 "The ___ Love" (R.E.M. hit)
68 Emphatic ending with yes

DOWN

1 Sends out junk email
2 French Revolution leader
3 Battery terminal
4 Kitchen gizmo
5 Tallest mountain in North America
6 Store (away)
7 Hilo greeting
8 Embassy workers
9 Unpleasant picnic surprise
10 Home to over three billion
11 New interpretation of an old song

12 Add up
13 Pig's digs
21 "___ won't!" (firm refusal)
22 Ad ___ committee
26 Suggestive
28 Willy Wonka's creator Roald
30 Book before Nehemiah
31 Darwin's concept
32 Olympic track event
33 Exasperates
35 Part of RSVP
36 Hosiery mishap
38 Flair
39 Get at in a hurry
40 Rock will beat them, but not paper
45 ___ Kan (dog food brand)
47 ___ chi
50 Bottled water brand
51 From that moment on
53 "___ come!"
54 *M*A*S*H* clerk
55 Words to the audience
56 "Yeah, sure. I bet."
58 Sicilian volcano
59 "The Little Red Hen" reply
60 *TV Guide* abbr.

75 *No More Left*

ACROSS

1 Coast Guard rank: Abbr.
4 Big name in hair care
11 Bushy do
14 Opposite of dep.
15 In the elements
16 Charged particle
17 Canada-wide wager?
19 CD-___
20 Obsess over, with "on"
21 Bodybuilders' bellies
22 Feint during a hockey game
23 At the ready
26 Starts to slip and slide?
28 Waltzing while sweeping the floor?
32 Job seeker's letter encl.
35 Mauna ___
36 Kind of down
37 Ante's place
38 "No more left" (and this puzzle's theme)
41 Always, in verse
42 Uproar
44 "Life ___ Highway" (Tom Cochrane)
45 Followers
46 Bumblebee's strategies?
50 Been aware of
51 Racy reading
55 Tony's Egyptian love
57 Yada, yada: Abbr.
59 Old hi-fis
60 Tic-tac-toe win
61 Gaseous godsends?
64 Bearded beast
65 Eroded
66 Tina's man
67 Pvt.'s superior
68 Residents of Damascus
69 D-Day transport: Abbr.

DOWN

1 "No ___" (impossible)
2 Big shrimp
3 "Coffee ___?"
4 Not as nerdy
5 Mon., in Montréal
6 One-time link
7 Madonna's "La ___ Bonita"
8 Poked fun at
9 Black Sea port
10 Reason to reserve at Wimbledon?
11 Yarn-spinning sites
12 Kasparov's castle
13 "Lean ___" (Withers)
18 Introduction to a monkey's uncle?
22 Prefix meaning "ten"
24 Rock's partner
25 Inept one, slangily
27 Dagger of old
29 Doug Henning's realm
30 Depilating cream
31 Guard dog's warnings
32 Sunblock stats
33 Juillet follower
34 Blow one's chances
38 T.O. CFLer
39 Prefix meaning "bone"
40 30-Down rival
43 ___ account (never)
45 "The world ___ much with us": Wordsworth
47 Sylvester's quarry
48 Hunting lodge coat-hook, maybe
49 Small jazz bands
52 How food is deep-fried
53 Dies, with "out"
54 It's a good thing
55 Gear teeth
56 Like Canadian winters
58 Roman 103
61 Half laughs
62 Actress Merkel
63 It's in the range: Abbr.

■ BARBARA OLSON & DAVE MACLEOD

1 ■ *À la Carte*

```
U S S R ■ J R S ■ ■ V O T E I N
N O T E B O O K ■ A M A N D A
B A R N E Y M I L L E R C O P
A M A T I S ■ J A U N T ■ ■
R I P E N ■ F U M E ■ ■ P S T
■ ■ G R U M P S G R I P E
P C B S ■ I S P ■ ■ R E L I C
S E A L E G S ■ W A R P A T H
A L I A S ■ G I T ■ S U S S
L I L Y L I V E R E D ■ ■
M A S ■ ■ N I N E ■ A P I P E
■ ■ G A S P E ■ A D O N I S
E S S A Y I S T C H A R L E S
T I N G E S ■ I N A S T A T E
A T L A S T ■ C R T ■ S W A N
```

2 ■ *Game Misconduct*

```
C H A R I S M A ■ O B L A D I
P A R A N O I D ■ P A U S E S
T H E R E S N O I I N T E A M
■ ■ I R A ■ S N A K E ■ ■
A G E N T ■ E C T O ■ M B A
U R N ■ G I G ■ H E N C O O P
F A R ■ A F O N D ■ ■ H O A R
■ N O T S I N C E I W E N T ■
L O L A ■ A R E N A ■ L E S
I L L I C I T ■ P E R ■ I R K
D A S ■ U N I V ■ P A T S Y
■ ■ S T A V E ■ P A S ■
T O T H E P E N A L T Y B O X
I R A I S E ■ O N E H O R S E
L A B A T T ■ M E A S U R E S
```

3 ■ *Capital Ideas*

```
L A R G E R ■ A H S O ■ S R I
O T O O L E ■ B O A S ■ N A N
C O O K I E D O U G H ■ A L C
■ M A S S E U S E ■ E R E I
I N F R A ■ N N E ■ A L L I T
S H U T ■ R E D C A B B A G E
I L L S E E ■ S A B B A T H S
■ ■ T M C ■ T O I ■ ■
H A N D H O L D ■ D E S C R Y
G R E E N P A R T Y ■ E A S E
W A C K O ■ M Y O ■ O L E O S
E L K E ■ M O L A S S E S ■
L S T ■ S C R A T C H C A K E
L E I ■ O X E N ■ T E T R A S
S A E ■ B I R D ■ V A S S A L
```

4 ■ *Black & White*

```
E T N A ■ S T O K E ■ O S L O
R O O M S T O L E T ■ R I E N
N E W S P A P E R S ■ E L S E
■ ■ O U T T A ■ T O A S T
C O Y ■ D U O ■ G L A S G O W
C O A R S E ■ B R A N ■ E N O
C O N E ■ B O O T I E ■ ■
■ K I L L E R W H A L E ■
■ N E U R O N ■ ■ M A R E
I T S ■ A N T S ■ A T S T U D
M I T Z V A H ■ M I A ■ S E A
P A R E E ■ C A S T E ■ ■
A R A B ■ P U Z Z L E G R I D
L A I R ■ T R A D E R O U T E
E S T A ■ L I R A S ■ S N I T
```

5 ■ *Crowd Noise*

6 ■ *Club of Jacks*

7 ■ *The Colour of Money*

8 ■ *Turn Up the Heat*

9 ■ *Cowboy Humour*

```
A C A S E ■ A P B ■ G O O D S
B A N A L ■ D R U ■ A P L E A
A V E M A R I A S ■ B E A S T
S O M E B O D Y T O L D ■
E R I ■ O N A ■ A M E ■ P M S
S T A I R ■ S A G E ■ A H O Y
■ A A S ■ B U G A B O O S
■ H I M T O G E T A L O N G ■
C A N B E R R A ■ S L R
P R O S ■ B E T A ■ A C A S T
R I N ■ T E A ■ R O B ■ N E W
■ L I T T L E D O G G I E
A S N A P ■ D I N E A L O N E
R O O F S ■ A K A ■ R E L E T
C O M F Y ■ Y E S ■ D E A R S
```

10 ■ *Turn Me Loose*

```
G A S ■ S T R A T A ■ O A S T
R I N ■ H A A G E N ■ R I P S
A M O ■ A T C O S T ■ D R I P
C A U G H T I N T H E A C T ■
E T T U ■ E L E C ■ C R A B S
■ L A D Y ■ A R S E N A L
■ I A M ■ B S M T ■ A L Y
H U N G U P T H E S A D D L E
E N C ■ S P A T ■ S R A
R E A L I S M ■ S A Y A ■
B A R O N ■ P A L L ■ N C O S
■ S N A G G E D A B I G O N E
S I A M ■ I R O N E D ■ L E E
P E T E ■ G E R T I E ■ T O M
F R E D ■ A D E S T E ■ S R S
```

11 ■ *A Day at the Office*

```
M A T I L D A ■ S E C A N T ■
A D A M A N T ■ P U L P E R ■
C O M P U T E R F R E E Z E ■
A S P ■ R O M E ■ O V A ■
W E A V E ■ P A P E R J A M
■ A L T I ■ S E R ■ U L E
S A U L ■ I G G Y ■ E A R E D
W A T E R C O O L E R B O R E
A R E T E ■ T O U R ■ A R T S
M G R ■ S S T ■ M O M S ■
P H O N E T A G ■ C H E F S
■ E T A ■ E M A G ■ N O I
E M P T Y C O F F E E U R N
D E A L I N ■ A R E A R U G
A L L E N S ■ S O S U E M E
```

12 ■ *Summer's Landscape*

```
S A T A N I C ■ T A M ■ M A T
C L A M A T O ■ I F A ■ A D D
R O T O T I L L E R S ■ R M S
A H E R O ■ L E I A ■ S K I ■
P A R E ■ L A W N M O W E R S
E S S ■ P E G ■ S E N A T E S
■ N I V E A ■ S T E R E
■ P R U N I N G S H E A R S ■
A R E M Y ■ R H E T T ■
R O W B O A T ■ A R S ■ W H O
G R E E N T H U M B ■ S E E D
A L D ■ H E L M ■ L U R I D
S T D ■ F E R T I L I Z E R S
E E E ■ O N A ■ E A T I N T O
L S D ■ E S P ■ S W E E T O N
```

13 ■ *Excellent!*

14 ■ *Start Groaning*

15 ■ *The Glass is Half Empty*

16 ■ *Prime Miniter*

17 ■ *Going Upscale*

18 ■ *Pour a Cold One*

19 ■ *Hurry Up and Wait*

20 ■ *Let's Rock*

21 ■ *Let's Roll*

22 ■ *Jumbled Words*

23 ■ *What's Missing, Eh?*

24 ■ *Just for the L of It*

25 ■ *Number Please*

26 ■ *Just Say Nay, or Nae, or . . .*

27 ■ *Nips at Noon*

28 ■ *Mixed Messages*

29 ■ *Misguided Youth*

I	T	S		H	A	Z	E	L		H	A	R	P	Y
C	O	O		A	S	I	D	E		E	I	E	I	O
E	B	B		L	I	N	G	O		A	R	S	O	N
B	A	B	Y	F	A	C	E	N	E	L	S	O	N	
A	G	E	E			S	I	N			L	E	A	
G	O	D	S	H	I	P		D	E	L	I	V	E	R
			H	E	L	L	O		I	N	E	R	T	
	B	I	L	L	Y	T	H	E	K	I	D			
B	R	A	V	O			T	O	L	E	T			
S	E	N	A	T	O	R		T	O	N	I	G	H	T
A	S	K		C	A	T			A	L	A	I		
	P	R	E	T	T	Y	B	O	Y	F	L	O	Y	D
P	E	A	C	H		G	O	N	E	R		A	N	I
A	C	T	O	R		U	N	C	L	E		T	E	E
S	T	E	N	O		N	E	E	L	Y		S	S	R

30 ■ *Now Here's a Switch*

C	O	O	N		R	E	H	E	A	T		M	S	G
A	U	T	O		P	L	E	N	T	Y		E	W	E
S	T	O	U	T	M	A	S	T	E	R		T	I	N
A	B	O	V	E		P	A	R	I		Z	A	N	E
S	I	L	E	N	T	S		U	N	F	O	L	D	
	D	E	A	D	S	E	A	S	T	R	O	L	L	S
			U	S	E		S	T	O	O	L	I	E	S
W	A	S				B	I	S			C	R	T	
E	T	C	E	T	E	R	A		T	A	S			
S	T	A	R	E	M	O	N	G	E	R	I	N	G	
	A	N	E	M	I	C		E	L	E	G	I	E	S
A	G	T	S		T	H	A	T		A	N	K	L	E
C	I	I			S	T	U	D	M	I	S	S	I	L	E
U	R	L		A	E	R	I	A	L		I	T	E	M
P	L	Y		D	R	E	A	D	S		N	A	D	A

31 ■ *Let It Snow!*

M	U	N	I	C	H		A	R	A	L		E	L	L
E	N	I	S	L	E		A	S	A	Y		T	O	O
O	H	T	H	E	W	E	A	T	H	E	R	O	U	T
W	I	E		A	I	R	S				E	N	D	S
S	P	R	I	N	T	S		K	A	R	T			
		B	U	T	T	H	E	F	I	R	E	I	S	
S	L	E	E	P		U	N	I	C	O	R	N	S	
K	E	G		A	S	N	O	T		O	R	R		
I	N	A	P	A	N	I	C		G	A	S	E	S	
S	O	D	E	L	I	G	H	T	F	U	L			
		K	I	L	N		A	L	M	A	N	A	C	
I	N	D	O		A	X	I	S		O	R	E		
S	I	D	E	I	S	F	R	I	G	H	T	F	U	L
A	G	A		S	H	A	G		H	O	W	E	L	L
W	H	Y		A	E	R	O		T	E	P	E	E	S

32 ■ *Where R You?*

O	F	G	A	B		F	O	R		C	S	P	O	T
L	O	O	F	A		U	P	A		A	T	A	R	I
D	R	U	I	D		N	E	V		S	A	S	E	S
B	A	G	G	I	N	G	R	I	G	H	T	S		
A	G	E		D	L	I			R	I	S	E	T	O
G	E	R	B	E	R		I	W	I	N		D	O	A
		B	A	B	B	L	I	N	G	B	O	O	K	
A	Z	U	L		T	I	N			E	N	T	S	
B	A	S	S	K	N	U	C	K	L	E	S			
U	N	E		N	A	S	H		E	A	S	E	L	S
T	E	R	R	O	R		A	S	S		L	O	A	
	B	A	C	K	A	L	L	E	Y	B	A	W	L	
P	R	A	N	K		F	Y	I		O	R	I	E	L
P	A	S	D	E		R	I	N		F	A	N	N	Y
S	H	E	R	D		O	N	E		F	E	E	D	S

33 ■ *I's in Here*

A	L	O	T		E	D	G	E		E	R	A	S	E
B	E	T	H		N	A	R	Y		M	U	L	E	S
C	A	R	R		F	R	E	E	F	O	R	A	L	L
S	H	O	O	T	I	N	G	S	I	T	A	R		
			W	A	N	E		O	N	E	L			
A	S	S	A	M		R	A	R	E	R		A	C	C
S	H	O	W	I	N		M	E	S		I	F	O	R
M	O	N	A	L	I	S	A	S	S	I	M	I	L	E
A	R	A	Y		C	T	S		E	S	P	R	I	T
D	E	R		L	E	A	S	H		I	L	E	N	E
			M	O	T	T		I	S	T	O			
	T	O	U	R	I	S	T	T	I	R	A	D	E	
I	T	O	L	D	Y	O	U	S	O		I	T	O	N
V	O	W	E	L		N	E	O	N		N	E	W	T
S	I	S	S	Y		S	Y	N	E		G	E	N	S

34 ■ *Let It B*E**

B	A	L	D	E	A	G	L	E		A	B	A	C	K
B	R	O	W	N	B	E	A	R		H	A	L	L	O
S	E	V	E	R	A	N	C	E		O	R	F	E	O
		E	L	O		E	T	C	E	T	E	R	A	
S	H	I	L	L	S		O	T	E		X	E	N	O
P	A	I	S	L	E	Y		G	R	A	D	E	D	
A	R	I		G	A	S	P		A	M	O	R	E	
		B	L	A	C	K	E	Y	E	S				
A	L	L	O	Y		K	I	L	O		P	L	Y	
C	O	A	X	E	D		E	L	M	T	R	E	E	
E	U	S	E		R	A	M		K	A	R	E	N	S
	T	A	L	L	U	L	A	H		D	I	S		
H	I	L	D	A		I	S	O	L	A	T	I	N	G
I	S	L	E	T		M	A	S	S	M	E	D	I	A
C	H	E	R	E		B	I	T	T	E	R	E	N	D

35 ■ *Odd Couples*

E	G	G	S		R	A	I	S	A		K	I	N	K
N	A	N	U		A	N	N	A	S		I	N	N	O
A	L	A	D		W	I	D	T	H		E	D	E	N
C	O	W	A	R	D	L	Y	B	R	A	V	E		
T	O	O	N	I	E		Y	A	W		N	A	P	
S	T	N		C	A	P	N		M	O	B	I	L	E
		F	O	L	L	O	W	S	L	E	A	D	S	
I	T	S	A		O	O	H		B	L	O	T		
P	A	T	I	E	N	T	N	U	R	S	E			
S	P	A	R	T	A		E	P	E	E		A	L	A
O	E	R		A	T	A		D	R	I	V	E	L	
	F	U	T	U	R	E	P	R	E	S	E	N	T	
S	L	I	P		R	O	D	E	O		A	N	N	E
C	E	S	T		A	M	I	E	S		I	G	O	R
H	I	H	O		L	A	T	K	E		D	E	N	S

36 ■ *K2 Expedition*

A	N	K	L	E		P	A	L		E	R	A	S
M	E	N	A	T		E	G	O		L	I	R	A
A	N	O	R	A	K		S	E	D	A	T	E	L	Y
N	E	C	K	L	A	C	E	S		S	O	L	O	S
A	S	K	S		R	O	T		K	I	N			
			C	A	S	A	B	A	S		L	T	D
	K	O	D	A	K		S	O	M	E	M	O	R	E
T	O	R	E	R	O	S		W	I	E	N	I	E	S
E	L	E	C	T	R	O	N		K	I	O	S	K
M	A	O		H	A	B	I	T	A	T			
		C	A	M		N	E	Z		A	K	I	M
I	D	T	A	G		P	E	D	E	S	T	A	L	S
T	U	R	G	E	N	E	V		S	T	A	Y	E	D
S	M	E	E		A	T	E		U	R	A	N	O
A	P	E	R		B	A	H		D	I	K	E	S

37 ■ *The Joke's on You*

38 ■ *Old Macdonald's Farm*

39 ■ *It's About Time*

40 ■ *Pipe Down!*

41 ■ Airborne Animals

```
T U N   L O B B E D   O P A L
O R E   O L E O L E   P O R E
P S T   K A R P O V   I R M A
J U M P I N G S P I D E R S
O L E O       E L I   I D I
B A N D B   U P S   V A D E R
    O M N I   R E G G A E
F L Y I N G S Q U I R R E L S
R E E S E S   U M P S
A T L A S   S E A   E L A T E
Y S L   U N O     O R I N
  L E A P I N G L I Z A R D S
M I D I   P A R A D E   O B I
E D A M   A T O N E S   W I G
G E T S   T A S K E T   S T N
```

42 ■ Inflation Pressure

```
E G G   A M O I   T O U T E D
P L O D D I N G   E N R A G E
H Y D R O G E N B A L L O O N
E P E E S   P O E S Y
S H E A   S I R E E   A P S E
    P R I C E E S T I M A T E
      V A C S   N E V E R
C O M R A D E   C B S N E W S
A P I A N   A H A T
S E L F A P P R A I S A L
K N E E   E A R T O   D E C K
    A T B A T   S A M O A
C A N A D I A N E C O N O M Y
C L O S E T   G L O M O N T O
S A L I N E   E S T E   S E S
```

43 ■ Play It Again

```
S H A N G H A I   S A M I A M
R U N A R I S K   A M A N D A
O N E T O T E N   R E G A I N
      E N O S   N I L E S
  C R O S S W O R D C L U E
S I L E N T E   U V S
P R O M O   U S E   S A D O
C O V E R T O P E R A T I O N
A N E T   H R S   S A M O A
    B E A   E A S T E R N
T O N G U E T W I S T E R
A N A R M   E E L S
N I C E L Y   D E E P E N D S
G O R G E D   G E T A L I F E
O N E G G S   E N S C O N C E
```

44 ■ How's Your Old Man?

```
I D I O T S   S K I L   R S A
D E S I R E   I N H E R I T S
A N A L O G   L E A N E D O N
    Y O U S K E D A D D L E
B A D   P E W       L E A
A L O S S   O N S   A R E S T
R O N I   P R A T T L E
B U T T E R E D P O P C O R N
    B O O T I E S   A P I E
G R E Y S   O A T   S P E C S
A E R     E L K   N E T
T W O F A T H E R O E S
S I D E D O O R   D I E S E L
B R E E D I N G   G N A R L Y
Y E S   S T E S   E S S A Y S
```

45 ■ *Prefix-ation*

46 ■ *Headake*

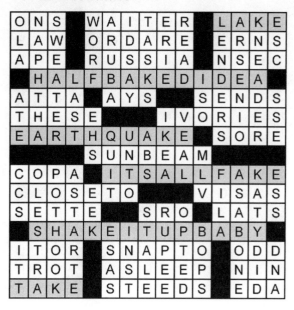

47 ■ *Pun Intended*

48 ■ *Governor General's Literary Award*

49 ■ *Seeing Things*

```
S S N . R E C A S T . E L E M
L I U . O R O M E O . G A G E
E C T . A L L S E T . G T O S
D E S I R E T O P O S S E S S
S M O R E . . . Y E A H S .
. . A R O N I . . R E T I E
E S C . B E V I G I L A N T
S L A V . L U I G I . L R O N
T A K E C A R E O F . T W A
O M E G A . S R T A S .
. . W A N N A . . S E C T S
G L A N C E B R I E F L Y A T
D E L I . N O T E L L . C R O
A S K S . E D E S S A . L T R
Y E S M . S E S T E T . E Y E
```

50 ■ *Give 'Em a Hand*

51 ■ *Somewhere a Dog Braked*

52 ■ *All in the Family*

```
A B E . A M E N D . E V A D E
M L S . R A R E E . L O V I N
B U T T E R S U P . L Y I N G
L E A V E I T T O B E A V E R
E S T A D O . S A N G .
D Y E D . Y S E R . E I R E
. . B R I E . K O U F A X
O Z Z I E A N D H A R R I E T
V E E R E D . A R T E .
A N D I . N A N S . R O O F
. . S P E C . S I E N N A
F A T H E R K N O W S B E S T
I L O S E . A E R O B A T I C
S O R E R . C O B R A . O D A
T U N A S . K N E E D . N E T
```

53 ■ *Get a Clue*

A	M	C		G	R	O	W	L	S		E	A	C	H
T	A	R		R	U	G	R	A	T		D	I	C	E
O	R	E		A	E	R	A	T	E		E	L	S	E
M	I	S	D	I	R	E	C	T	I	O	N			
S	A	T	A	N			K	E	N	T		R	A	G
			G	I	B	E			S	T	A	R	E	
F	L	A	G	E	L	L	A	T	E		A	B	E	T
L	A	T	E	R	A	L	T	H	I	N	K	I	N	G
O	N	O	R		H	A	V	E	N	E	E	D	T	O
S	A	L	S	A			M	E	T	A				
S	I	L		A	D	E	S			W	I	P	E	S
			T	H	E	A	H	A	M	O	M	E	N	T
B	O	N	E		G	R	A	T	E	R		T	E	A
I	S	E	E		A	T	R	E	S	T		A	R	M
B	O	O	N		S	H	E	E	S	H		L	O	P

54 ■ *Stressing Out!*

C	A	R	T	S		T	A	B	S		S	T	E	P
A	G	A	I	N		A	N	E	T		U	H	O	H
R	E	N	E	E		I	T	T	Y		M	E	N	D
E	N	T	R	A	N	C	E	E	X	A	M	S		
E	D	O		K	U	H	N			R	E	P	A	S
N	A	N	A		M	I	N	U	T	E	R	I	C	E
			L	E	B		A	B	A	T		A	T	E
S	E	D	A	T	E	S		C	L	O	W	N	E	D
A	R	I		E	S	T	E		K	O	A			
D	E	S	E	R	T	R	A	T	S		S	M	O	G
A	S	H	E	N		R	E	A	L		I	N	A	
	P	R	E	S	E	N	T	T	E	N	S	E	S	
C	H	A	I		O	V	E	R		T	O	A	D	S
P	I	N	E		N	A	S	A		B	U	D	G	E
U	S	S	R		E	N	T	S		E	N	D	E	D

55 ■ *Vowel Play*

F	O	I	L		P	E	A	S		E	L	A	T	E
I	N	T	E	R	R	U	P	T		B	O	W	E	N
D	A	G	W	O	O	D	B	U	M	S	T	E	A	D
O	N	O		S	N	O			R	E	S			
			D	E	G	R	E	E	I	N	A	R	T	S
S	A	R	I			A	A	A			E	E	E	
O	R	A	N	G	E		S	C	R	E	A	M	E	D
D	I	G	G	I	N	G	T	H	E	S	C	E	N	E
D	O	T	O	A	T	E	E		D	E	A	L	E	R
E	S	A			R	R	S			S	T	R	S	
D	O	G	G	O	N	E	S	H	A	M	E			
			L	M	N		E	L	L		S	E	T	
D	U	G	O	N	E	S	E	L	F	A	H	O	L	E
A	T	A	R	I		P	A	L	I	S	A	D	E	S
B	A	B	Y	S		F	U	S	E		D	A	M	S

56 ■ *Boo!*

S	U	B	T	L	E		I	N	O	W		S	S	E
A	G	R	E	E	D		C	O	P	A		A	N	N
G	H	O	S	T	W	R	I	T	E	R		R	A	M
		W	T	S		A	N	O	N		I	N	R	E
E	O	N	S		D	I	E	F		T	A	I	L	S
N	B	C		M	O	N	S	T	E	R	M	A	S	H
G	O	O	G	O	O		S	E	D	A	N			
R	E	W	A	R	D	S		N	I	C	O	S	I	A
			S	P	A	M	S		S	E	T	T	E	R
W	I	T	C	H	D	O	C	T	O	R		R	R	R
I	T	W	A	S		T	A	R	N		V	E	E	S
C	H	O	P		T	H	R	U		T	I	A		
K	I	A		S	K	E	L	E	T	O	N	K	E	Y
E	N	C		P	O	R	E		A	C	C	E	D	E
T	K	T		A	S	S	T		S	K	I	R	U	N

57 ■ Vowel Play 2

```
D E L C O   S A P I D   O R E
A L O O F   E V E R I   F I T
B A G O F T R I C K S   A L E
S N O   S A I S     P Y R E S
    B E G F O R M E R C Y
R A N A T     E A R S
O M A N   I T S A Y S   E B B
B I G G E R A N D B E T T E R
S S S   V A L L E E   E T N A
    M A N O     S E E D S
    B O G G I N G D O W N
V E R S A   O R H E   Y S L
O T S   B U G S Y M A L O N E
U A E   O R S E A   T O G A S
S S R   R I T E S   S O A P S
```

58 ■ Sweep!

```
E S S A Y   R O M   A M I E L
A P P R E H E N D   H E D G E
S O F T R O C K S T A T I O N
E T S   T O U P E E   R E S T
      A L D     C H I
    T A K E O U T C H I C K E N
S A R I   O N R U S H   E S E
H E I N Z   A U T   O S A K A
A B O   E S P R I T   U N I T
H O T B U T T O N I S S U E
      U S A     M P S
S O A R   S L A V E R   R O B
S K I P T H E C E R E M O N Y
R O D E O   G O E S A F T E R
S K E D S   S P R   D R O I D
```

59 ■ A Chilling Deduction

```
C L A N   U S A F   H E A R T
O I L Y   P A R I   E N N U I
C A M E R A M E N   L E D I N
A M A T H T E A C H E R I N
    S Y R     H O N G
K I T   T E N S   L E E W A Y
A N U N H E A T E D   T I N A
P H N O M   T O R   A I D E R
P E E K   R O O M I S C O L D
A R R I V E   D A S H   W E S
    D A B S     O R S
  A N D C A L C U L A T I N G
L U C I A   U R S A M I N O R
B R A N T   M E E T   C A N I
S A R G E   P E R E   K N O T
```

60 ■ On the Sly

```
I N O R   E L A T E D   L U G
N O N E   X A N A D U   O N O
A B E L   A L D R I N   O L A
W I L E E C O Y O T E   M E T
E G B E R T     S A L A
      R A G B A G   B A R T
A S T R O   A R L O   O R N O
T H E A R T F U L D O D G E R
E O N S   O F I T   W E E D Y
M E A T   R E N O W N
    S C A R     A U R O R A
G T I   S N E A K Y P E T E S
O O O   V E S T A L   H E M I
T R U   P A T I N A   A R I D
H E S   S P O T T Y   B I T E
```

61 ■ *Food for Thought*

C	A	S	T		A	S	I	A	N		A	M	P	S
O	C	T	A		S	E	T	T	O		S	E	E	P
M	C	A	N		T	R	O	T	S		E	M	E	R
B	U	R	G	E	R	F	R	I	E	S	C	O	K	E
A	S	T	O	N			R	D	A		R	E	A	
T	E	S		E	V	A	D	E		W	E	I	R	D
		A	R	O	L	E			N	A	S	S		
	C	H	O	L	E	S	T	E	R	O	L			
S	U	R	E			K	I	T	E	S				
I	T	E	M	S		A	S	P	E	N		A	I	R
A	T	V		K	E	N			T	I	T	H	E	
M	E	A	T	A	N	D	P	O	T	A	T	O	E	S
E	R	S	E		D	R	O	N	E		A	M	A	T
S	E	S	E		E	E	R	I	E		L	I	R	E
E	D	E	N		D	I	E	T	S		S	C	A	D

62 ■ *Tons of Fun*

W	O	R	M	S		F	L	A	W		O	O	Z	Y
A	L	O	O	N		R	E	D	H	A	I	R	E	D
L	A	Y	T	O	N	A	W	A	Y	P	L	A	N	S
		H	O	O	P		P	S	T	S				
G	O	E	S	T	O	P	O	T				C	T	R
A	N	D		N	E	W	T	O	N	B	O	R	N	
G	R	U	E	L		S	N	O	W	T	I	R	E	S
	A	C	E	I	N			E	W	E	R	S		
S	M	A	R	M	I	E	S	T		T	N	U	T	S
U	P	T	O	P	A	R	T	O	N		P	L	O	
E	S	E		A	U	T	O	M	A	T	E	D		
	S	E	T	S		A	V	I	S					
W	A	L	K	T	H	E	P	L	A	N	K	T	O	N
I	N	R	E	S	E	R	V	E		I	M	O	F	F
N	O	T	E		E	S	T	D		S	E	G	A	L

63 ■ *Focus on Solvers*

S	R	T	A	S		S	C	R	A	M		M	T	S
H	A	R	D	C		P	R	I	C	E		A	S	A
E	V	A	D	E		R	O	T	O	R		N	H	L
S	E	C	O	N	D		S	U	R		S	N	I	T
		N	E	E	D	S	A	N	S	W	E	R	S	
D	I	B	S		J	O	W	L		T	A	R	T	
O	S	O		M	A	K	O		S	E	M	I		
C	R	U	C	I	V	E	R	B	A	L	I	S	T	S
	N	A	N	U		D	O	T	E		M	A	O	
	L	D	R	S		S	P	R	Y		I	S	I	S
B	L	A	N	K	S	Q	U	A	R	E	S			
W	A	R	Y		C	U	Z		S	L	A	L	O	M
A	M	I		C	R	A	Z	E		L	Y	I	N	G
N	A	E		C	E	L	L	O		E	S	K	E	R
A	S	S		S	E	L	E	S		N	O	E	L	S

64 ■ *Two in One*

S	C	T	V		S	H	A	L	E		A	W	A	R
E	L	O	I		H	O	P	E	D		S	E	L	A
T	I	L	L		A	O	R	T	A		E	L	L	E
T	E	L	L	A	G	R	I	M	M	T	A	L	E	
O	N	E	A	M		A	L	E		A	T	T	Y	S
S	T	R		U	G	H		O	R	T		O	O	O
		T	S	O		S	U	E		I	D	O	S	
	M	A	K	E	A	P	I	T	T	S	T	O	P	
L	O	C	O		P	A	N		I	W	A			
A	R	R		F	E	U		G	E	E		S	M	A
S	T	O	M	A		N	G	O		E	T	H	Y	L
	A	B	E	T	A	C	A	R	R	T	H	E	F	T
P	L	A	N		C	H	I	D	E		A	L	O	E
A	L	T	A		H	E	L	I	O		I	V	O	R
S	Y	S	T		E	S	S	E	S		S	E	T	S

65 ■ *Feeling Grand*

A	T	I	T		L	A	P	O	F		B	E	D	E
R	O	S	S		O	N	E	A	L		A	P	E	X
T	O	R	A		S	E	T	T	O		A	S	A	P
	L	A	R	G	E	R	T	H	A	N	L	I	F	E
M	A	E			P	R	A	Y	S	T	O		L	E	N
A	T	L	A	S					I	R	O	N	S	
W	E	I	R		H	O	R	S	E	S	E	N	S	E
		O	V	E	R	S	I	Z	E	D				
S	E	A	M	O	N	S	T	E	R		I	A	G	O
I	N	L	A	W					A	D	L	I	B	
A	T	L		E	M	O	T	E	R	S		M	R	I
M	E	G	A	L	O	M	A	N	I	A	C	A	L	
E	R	O	S		V	E	R	S	O		U	N	I	T
S	E	N	T		I	N	P	U	T		B	A	S	K
E	D	E	R		E	S	S	E	S		E	C	H	O

66 ■ *The Walloping Gourmet*

D	I	E	T	S		I	R	E		S	A	I	D	A
E	G	G	B	E	A	T	E	R		E	Z	R	A	S
L	O	O	S	E	L	I	P	S		M	T	I	D	A
				F	I	N	I		T	I	E	S	O	N
H	A	W	A	I	I	A	N	P	U	N	C	H		
A	L	I	S	T			O	N	U	S				
T	A	S	K		E	C	H	O	E	D		L	A	O
C	R	E	A	M	S	H	O	R	T	E	N	I	N	G
H	M	S		I	C	A	N	S	O		E	C	O	L
			C	L	A	M				O	X	I	D	E
	W	H	I	P	P	E	D	B	U	T	T	E	R	
C	O	Y	O	T	E		X	O	U	T				
O	H	A	R	A		I	C	E	L	A	N	D	E	R
O	T	T	E	R		P	O	R	K	C	H	O	P	S
P	O	T	S	Y		O	N	S		T	A	C	I	T

67 ■ **Empty Promises*

B	E	F	I	T		P	E	A		R	I	A	L	S
A	M	I	N	O		A	L	L		E	N	T	E	R
K	I	L	T	S		P	A	T	E	N	T	E	E	S
E	L	L	A		T	A	N	A	G	E	R			
R	E	S	C	U	E		D	R	A	W	A			
		I	T	S	S	O			D	A	N	C	E	D
L	E	N		A	T	R	I	A		L	E	A	V	E
O	A	T	S			E	T	Y			T	R	E	F
U	S	H	E	R		S	T	E	W	S		T	R	Y
T	E	E	T	E	R		S	A	P	O	R			
		S	T	A	R	E		L	A	R	I	A	T	
		C	A	R	A	M	E	L		I	D	L	E	
P	R	U	R	I	E	N	C	E		B	E	G	I	N
O	A	K	E	N		G	E	L		E	L	E	C	T
W	H	E	W	S		Y	E	S		E	S	S	E	S

68 ■ *What Lies Beneath*

A	A	H	E	D		S	H	A		T	B	O	N	E
G	R	O	V	E		T	O	P		E	R	O	S	E
A	C	L	A	M		A	B	E	R	R	A	N	C	E
S	H	A	D	O	W	B	O	X	E	R	S			
P	E	S	E	T	A				P	O	S	H	E	R
			R	A	D	I	A	T	O	R	H	O	S	E
N	I	T		P	E	R	M	I	T		A	N	K	A
A	N	O	D	E		E	O	E		S	T	O	I	C
I	T	T	O		A	N	O	R	A	K		R	E	T
F	R	E	U	D	I	A	N	S	L	I	P			
S	O	M	B	E	R				S	P	A	R	T	A
	L	A	T	E	B	L	O	O	M	E	R	S		
B	L	U	E	R	O	D	E	O		V	E	N	U	S
B	E	A	U	T		D	A	B		E	L	I	S	E
L	O	W	P	H		Y	D	S		R	A	N	T	S

69 ■ *About Face*

D	I	D	N	T	■	A	T	O	I	■	L	O	O	T
I	S	O	U	R	■	B	R	A	N	■	O	L	L	A
S	H	U	T	E	■	B	A	R	T	E	N	D	E	R
C	O	S	M	E	T	I	C	S	U	R	G	E	O	N
S	T	E	E	L	I	E	■	■	R	I	S	■	■	■
■	■	■	G	E	T	■	L	U	N	K	H	E	A	D
A	A	A	■	S	A	D	A	T	■	■	O	M	N	I
I	T	W	A	S	N	I	P	A	N	D	T	U	C	K
L	I	A	M	■	■	A	S	H	O	E	■	S	E	E
S	T	R	A	D	D	L	E	■	L	M	N	■	■	■
■	■	■	Z	O	O	■	■	S	T	O	U	T	E	R
S	T	R	E	T	C	H	T	H	E	T	R	U	T	H
T	O	A	D	S	T	O	O	L	■	A	S	T	H	E
E	M	M	A	■	O	N	M	E	■	P	E	T	I	T
W	E	P	T	■	R	E	S	P	■	E	D	I	C	T

70 ■ *Up For Grabs*

S	W	I	F	T	■	C	A	B	S	■	L	A	D	Y
T	I	T	L	E	■	A	G	R	A	■	E	I	R	E
A	N	N	A	N	■	R	E	A	R	E	N	D	E	R
T	O	O	K	T	H	E	S	T	A	N	D	■	■	■
S	S	W	■	O	A	F	■	T	H	E	L	E	F	T
■	■	■	T	R	A	Y	■	■	■	B	R	O	■	■
A	B	E	R	D	E	E	N	■	S	H	O	O	I	N
C	A	P	T	U	R	E	D	T	H	E	F	L	A	G
C	U	S	S	E	S	■	S	E	E	S	T	A	R	S
R	E	O	■	■	M	O	A	B	■	■	■	■	■	■
A	R	M	O	I	R	E	■	R	A	G	■	A	C	E
■	■	■	S	E	I	Z	E	D	T	H	E	D	A	Y
F	O	O	T	R	A	C	E	R	■	O	L	D	I	E
A	X	L	E	■	T	A	R	O	■	U	S	E	N	O
R	O	A	R	■	A	L	O	P	■	L	A	D	E	N

71 ■ *Whose What?*

G	A	L	■	B	R	E	N	T	■	D	A	U	N	T
R	O	O	■	M	E	M	O	S	■	I	N	D	U	E
I	R	R	■	O	L	I	V	E	R	S	T	O	N	E
E	T	E	■	V	E	L	A	■	O	R	I	■	■	■
F	A	T	C	I	T	Y	■	T	O	U	C	H	U	P
■	■	T	O	E	S	■	S	I	M	P	S	O	N	S
L	I	A	R	S	■	S	P	L	I	T	■	W	A	S
E	R	S	E	■	W	H	I	T	E	■	D	A	R	T
D	A	W	■	B	I	E	R	S	■	F	I	R	M	S
U	N	I	T	E	D	L	Y	■	M	R	E	D	■	■
C	I	T	A	D	E	L	■	B	E	A	T	S	M	E
■	■	■	M	T	S	■	E	A	R	N	■	T	A	G
R	O	B	E	R	T	S	T	A	C	K	■	E	N	G
E	X	T	R	A	■	S	T	E	E	L	■	R	I	O
M	O	U	S	Y	■	R	E	D	R	Y	■	N	A	N

72 ■ *Chill Out*

R	A	C	E	■	T	S	O	■	I	M	P	O	R	T
A	L	O	T	■	O	P	P	■	S	O	A	R	E	R
F	I	N	D	A	Q	U	I	E	T	P	L	A	C	E
E	T	C	■	R	U	D	E	R	■	■	A	T	A	N
■	■	■	A	N	T	E	■	I	C	E	C	O	L	D
C	A	R	E	■	S	A	T	■	O	V	E	R	L	Y
A	S	N	A	P	■	V	O	I	C	E	■	■	■	■
W	H	E	R	E	Y	O	U	C	A	N	R	E	S	T
■	■	■	N	E	W	T	O	■	T	I	G	E	R	■
C	A	B	A	N	A	■	E	N	G	■	O	G	L	E
R	E	A	D	E	R	S	■	■	A	N	T	H	■	■
A	R	C	H	■	E	N	E	R	O	■	E	G	O	■
T	A	K	E	A	D	E	E	P	B	R	E	A	T	H
E	T	E	R	N	E	■	R	E	L	■	E	D	O	M
S	E	R	E	N	E	■	F	E	E	■	S	S	S	S

73 ■ *Yes, Yes, Yes!*

M	E	C	C	A		P	R	O	F		R	O	O	K
A	V	R	I	L		R	E	P	O		A	C	N	E
T	E	E	T	O	T	A	L	E	R		T	E	R	N
		A	Y	E	A	Y	E	C	A	P	T	A	I	N
S	S	T		P	E	T		S	E	A	N	C	E	
P	O	I	N	T	E	R		C	O	U	N	S	E	L
A	L	O	S	S		E	I	N						
T	E	N	F	O	U	R	B	I	G	B	U	D	D	Y
			N	O	B			S	N	O	R	E		
L	A	T	T	I	C	E		L	A	S	A	G	N	A
A	S	W	I	R	L		D	I	X		T	O	R	
O	K	I	L	E	E	D	O	K	I	L	E	E		
T	O	N	E		S	O	R	E	L	O	S	E	R	S
S	U	E	R		A	N	I	L		O	T	T	O	S
E	T	D	S		M	A	C	Y		T	A	H	O	E

74 ■ *Aah, Summertime!*

S	M	A	R	M		S	A	A	B		A	R	M	S
P	A	N	I	C		A	L	I	E		S	E	A	T
A	R	O	C	K		L	O	D	E		I	N	K	Y
M	A	D	E	I	N	T	H	E	S	H	A	D	E	
S	T	E	R	N	O		A	S	T	O		I	S	R
			L	I	D			I	C	E	T	E	A	
	E	D	I	E		A	S	S	N		Z	I	N	C
E	V	E	R	Y	T	H	I	N	G	S	R	O	S	Y
L	O	C	K		E	L	L	A		C	A	N	E	
A	L	A	S	K	A			G	T	I				
N	U	T		A	R	E	S		A	S	H	R	A	M
	T	H	E	L	I	V	I	N	I	S	E	A	S	Y
T	I	L	T		N	I	N	O		O	R	D	I	E
B	O	O	N		T	A	C	T		R	E	A	D	Y
A	N	N	A		O	N	E	I		S	I	R	E	E

75 ■ *No More Left*

C	P	O		C	L	A	I	R	O	L		F	R	O
A	R	R		O	U	T	S	I	D	E		I	O	N
N	A	T	I	O	N	A	L	B	E	T		R	O	M
D	W	E	L	L		A	B	S		D	E	K	E	
O	N	A	L	E	R	T		E	S	S	E	S		
		B	R	O	O	M	D	A	N	C	I	N	G	
S	A	S	E		L	O	A		E	I	D	E	R	
P	O	T		A	L	L	G	O	N	E		E	E	R
F	U	R	O	R		I	S	A		I	S	T	S	
S	T	I	N	G	T	A	C	T	I	C	S			
	K	N	O	W	N		E	R	O	T	I	C	A	
C	L	E	O		E	T	C		M	O	N	O	S	
O	O	O		H	E	L	I	U	M	B	O	O	N	S
G	N	U		A	T	E	I	N	T	O		I	K	E
S	G	T		S	Y	R	I	A	N	S		L	S	T

MORE
O Canada Crosswords!

With their distinctive folk-art covers and uniquely Canadian content, the *O Canada Crosswords* books have garnered a devoted fan base of crossword aficionados from coast to coast. Spellings are Canadian too, and the words are derived from our history, geography and pop culture.

O Canada Crosswords, Book 1, 115 Great Canadian Crosswords • 8½ x 11, 136 pp, pb
978-1-894404-02-0 • $14.95
O Canada Crosswords, Book 2, 50 Giant Weekend-size Crosswords • 8½ x 11, 120 pp, pb
978-1-894404-04-4 • $14.95
O Canada Crosswords, Book 3, 50 More Giant Weekend Crosswords • 8½ x 11, 120 pp, pb
978-1-894404-11-2 • $14.95
O Canada Crosswords, Book 4, 50 Incredible Giant Weekend Crosswords • 8½ x 11, 120 pp, pb
978-1-894404-18-1 • $14.95
O Canada Crosswords, Book 5, 50 Fantastic Giant Weekend Crosswords • 8½ x 11 • 120 pp, pb
978-1-894404-20-4 • $14.95
O Canada Crosswords, Book 6, 50 Great Weekend-size Crosswords • 8½ x 11 • 120 pp, pb
978-0-88971-206-5 • $14.95
O Canada Crosswords, Book 7, 50 Wonderful Weekend-size Crosswords • 8½ x 11 • 120 pp, pb
978-0-88971-218-8 • $14.95